Africa
Through Structuration
Theory – *ntu*

Jean Pierre Elonga Mboyo

Langaa Research & Publishing CIG
Mankon, Bamenda

Publisher:
Langaa RPCIG
Langaa Research & Publishing Common Initiative Group
P.O. Box 902 Mankon
Bamenda
North West Region
Cameroon
Langaagrp@gmail.com
www.langaa-rpcig.net

Distributed in and outside N. America by African Books Collective
orders@africanbookscollective.com
www.africanbookscollective.com

ISBN: 9956-762-96-2

DISCLAIMER
All views expressed in this publication are those of the author and do not
necessarily reflect the views of Langaa RPCIG.

Acknowledgement

Some people set out to write a book. You can tell as you read the first chapter and come across the 'hindsight' reference in the last chapter that this book project formed as my writing developed. Either way, other people around you play a part. I am therefore grateful for all the support I got from everyone whenever I needed my many drafts to be proofread, critiqued for readability, overall clarity and coherence. Though some have chosen to remain anonymous, I thank others at the end of the chapters wherever appropriate. All that is left is for me to express my sincere gratitude to my friend Vincent Asambom who, in our many a discussion, challenged some of my ideas and in the process enabled me to crystallise some of my thoughts.

Dedication

To my beloved and patient wife Marina and adorable children Verison, Fasia Cecille and Tyrell Elonga.

My wife and I set out to build the institution called family. When our children came along, each in their uniqueness, they transformed 'the family' and together our family is both the medium and product of everyone's presence (That is what this book Africa through Structuration Theory – *ntu* is also about).

Table of Contents

Preface

In the book chapter *'The movement towards democracy: global, continental and state perspectives'*, Wiseman (2002:2) makes the following remark about continental Africa: 'Africa is not a major actor on the world stage: in both military and economic terms it is extremely weak by global standard'. In this publication *'Africa through Structuration Theory – ntu'*, I seek therefore to solve an enduring problem of poverty – whether chronic or transitory (Aliber 2003), underdevelopment and unfulfilled hopes on the African continent. I do so by drawing attention to leadership. In my view, such a challenging project could not be successfully executed unless it is planted against the backdrop of a fitting understanding of how social phenomenon is constructed. Structuration theory of Antony Giddens (1979; 1984), therefore, serves as a stepping stone to conceptualise various (African) historical facts with regard to both structure and agency and analyses have led me to propose *duality of structures* as a solution to current leadership problems.

It is important that a brief narrative is provided just to remind ourselves about the nature of the problem before I elaborate on how specific issues that are discussed here interlink. Africa, whenever and wherever one starts looking at it, can be framed as a geographical location where the majority of people live in poverty despite the wealth around them. There is talk of renewed investment interests on the continent but, if they flourish, such success would be coming out on the heels of a devastating past. The paradox of 'poverty despite wealth' is common. In *West Africa Hosts*

Untapped Mineral Wealth, the anonymous author (2010) describes Burkina Faso as hosting

> some of the richest untapped geographical wealth on the African continent. But due to a history of political instability, military coups, extreme drought and unfavourable investment legislation, it is not surprising that, until recently both majors and juniors alike have steered clear of the country' (54).

About Niger, it is remarked that 'the country has suffered a troubled political history and remains desperately poor' (56) despite its uranium and other minerals such as gold. About Liberia, the author mentions its iron ore:

> Iron ore exports accounted for more than half of the country's total export income and it was a major source of local employment. That iron industry was abruptly interrupted by civil war and continual fighting between 1989 and 2003. Violence left the war-torn nation crippled and poor, even by West Africa standards (57).

And finally about Guinea-Conakry, the author highlights that the country is home to 30% of the world's bauxite reserves before highlighting its iron ore and gold deposits. Despite this wealth and the recent 2010 'democratic elections' in the country, peace is still precarious and the country still has to find a way out of poverty that resulted partly from the authoritarian rule it was plunged into just after independence from France in 1958.

On the energy front, a lot still needs to be achieved. While the African population is predicted to grow by 71% by

2035, increase in energy supply is expected at only 38%. This is bound to trigger questions given the fact that continental Africa

> has an abundance of natural gas and oil in northern and western Africa, an abundance of coal in southern Africa, and abundance of water resources in central Africa. Continental Africa can be regarded as one giant solar panel, and wind is plentiful in the arid desert and coastal regions. There is no shortage of energy resources, traditional or renewable. (Naidoo and Bacela 2012: 67-68)

The list of devastating stories is endless but there are some success stories too. The personal and institutional struggles against apartheid by the late noble peace prize laureate and former South African president Nelson Mandela stand out as one. However, more than a decade on since Wiseman (2002) put the comment used to begin this introductory preface into print, stories of dashed hopes and missed opportunities continue to plague the continent so much so that the following observation by Antony Giddens is as valid today as it was then: 'in some African countries, living standards have fallen not just in relative terms but in absolute ones too' (Giddens 2002: xxvii).

The situation is hopeless that one wonders if Africa is predetermined to live in this way just as a dog is predetermined to eat bones. But here I am reminded of the Akan proverb (Ghana & Ivory Coast) that reads: 'Dogs do not actually prefer bones to meat; it is just no one ever gives them meat'. The largely youthful popular uprising that shook Tunisia, Egypt, Burkina Faso, the Democratic Republic of Congo (DRC)...can be seen as a show of Africa's determination to be recognised as a democratic and economic force on the world stage, moments when dogs refused to be fed with bones.

This publication attempts to offer a way out of the limbo that we are in through a hopefully rigorous theoretical conceptualisation which identifies leadership as a problem in Africa, offers research ideas and application of Giddens' structuration theory of duality of structures. Some might view my approach as abstract and idealistic. Firstly, when discussing matters that touch on the essence of a particular people (Africans in this case), philosophy and abstraction impose themselves instead of it being a purely sterile academic indulgence unworthy of the seriousness of this publication. Secondly, the author sees it as a practical guide that uses concrete examples and effectively links abstraction to real situations. While the leadership examples of the likes of Nelson Mandela can presumably be regarded as prototypes of what the author is advocating, its future success admittedly depends on willing agents and structures that are honest enough to acknowledge the limits of old practices and give innovation a chance.

This book is therefore a conceptual enterprise that relies on secondary sources rather than first hand fieldwork in Africa. In other words, this is a duality-of-structures inspired agenda-setting conceptual analysis which is largely based on a mixture of evidence from publications around the topics such as: politics, environment, democracy, conflict, leadership theories; methodological concepts; biographical illustrations; and the author's reflective diary. It does not depart from a tried and tested example of duality of structures to claim that this IS the way out of poverty. What it does however is to provide (a) model analytical framework (s) for conceptualising current social problems/challenges in Africa and ignite a secondary-evidence based reflection on what leadership (and other related concepts) in Africa should be understood in order to revert the current narrative of poverty. To that extent structuration theory CAN be a way out of poverty.

Based on the above understanding, it is expected that you, as a reader, would begin to wonder whether the argument this publication makes is either deductive or inductive. It is both and let me explain why I have come to that conclusion. Sidestepping individual preferences on the validity or veracity of either deductive or inductive methods (Tsang and Williams 2012), *Africa through Structuration Theory – ntu* can be viewed from a deductive point of view. It begins from a general sociological theory in order to understand a particular African context, even though the idea of a homogenous African context is somewhat problematic.

However, holding the argument as this publication hopefully does through the use of examples from various African countries supports the view here of a 'common' African context. Starting from an explicit theory (Structuration Theory) does not necessarily mean that the study is exclusively deductive and not inductive. Kimoyo (2008), Smeulers and Hoex (2010), that I refer to later on, do not explicitly frame their study from Giddens' theory but, in reality, the studies' findings are based on an oscillation between citizens (agents) and governmental institutions' (structure) struggles that lead to the barbaric acts during the Rwandan genocide, for example. Since induction starts from particular examples to argue a (general) theory, one might accept structure and agency inferences from Kimoyo and Smeulers and Hoex's studies as one example. Not to view *Africa through Structuration Theory - ntu* as an inductive enterprise despite its integration of examples from across Africa is simply an attempt to arbitrarily subordinate secondary sources to primary sources.

The inclusion of examples (mainly from Africa), regardless of the order of importance that the reader attributes to either primary or secondary sources, should be enough reassurance that this publication is not based on assumptions which can be understood to be 'statements about phenomena that are accepted as valid without submission to tests of their validity' (Dixon 1977:119) or without proof (Oxford English Dictionary). That said; the book is divided as follows:

Chapter 1 "*African-Centred Leadership and the Theory of Structuration: a response to Obiakor*" presents one of the ways that has been suggested to resolve an enduring problem of poverty on the African continent. It analyses the arguments presented by Obiakor (2004) and using Giddens' structuration theory, the chapter concludes with a slightly different approach to tackling the plight of Africans. The new perspective being suggested here requires to be seen not only as a reaction to a different approach but also as a philosophy in its own right, hence the second chapter which serves as the foundation for this chapter and subsequent ones.

Chapter 2 '*Structure and agency dichotomy: an issue of trust?*' reviews structure and agency debate, brings some contemporary examples from Europe but mainly from Africa, and suggests that structure and agency have broken each other's trust and only a philosophy based on *duality of structures* could restore the broken trust between them.

Chapter 3 '*Duality of structures: a, not THE, methodology*' discusses the ontological, epistemological, ethical and other issues specifically related to Africa. In chapter 1 'African-centred leadership and the theory of structuration: a response to Obiakor', I suggest that *Increasing self-scrutiny on the part of leaders and decreasing fear on the part of the population* are the duo indicators of a healthy exercise of duality of structures to restore the broken trust between structure and agency. In re-examining the African conception of ontology, epistemology and methodology, the author wonders whether Structuration Theory is in effect an 'authentically' African Theory. But if the analysis does not convince you as a reader, the author recognises it as an entrenched belief that anything remotely associated with the West is 'foreign' and therefore unsuitable in a different African setting. This issue questions this entire publication which effectively uses Antony Giddens' (British) social theory on African context. The following chapter discusses this in more detail.

Chapter 4 '*Double de-contextualisation: a methodological myth or reality?*' engages with issues of how an African and others who may (or may not) be thought to be at the centre or peripheries of knowledge, apply theories that can be said to be bounded within some contextual structures such as Europe/Africa when engaged in research. The age of modernity has increased mobility and blurred boundaries, it is therefore essential that a repertoire of arguments is developed to justify the use of otherwise 'foreign' ideas on the Africa continent. There is an element of academic freedom argued not from a human rights perspective but from a scientific point of view instead.

The final chapter '*Higher education in the DRC and Sub Saharan Africa: an example of duality of structures in action*' discusses higher education in the DRC and Sub-Saharan Africa. Unlike the methodology chapter which sheds light on how to carry out research based on duality of structures, this chapter proposes a leadership and curriculum design framework for universities in the DRC and Sub-Saharan Africa which stand as an example of duality of structures in action.

It is only due to my professional and academic background in education that I discuss 'universities' here as an example. Otherwise, several other examples in fields such as health, judiciary, religion, business and media in various parts of the continent could be (have been) investigated. There are undoubtedly such initiatives already and many more will certainly continue to address specific issues of poverty reduction from various perspectives in different fields. However, what this publication also does is to highlight the need for (a) converging conceptual framework (s) that would guide such actions.

African wisdom has it that;

'If you want to go quickly (*or nowhere* – my italics), go alone. If you want to go far, go together' – African proverb.

The above proverb sums up the thinking that is being proposed throughout the chapters, that of the need for interaction between structure and agency.

I hope to be read by all those who care about the plight of millions of Africans whose homeland have turned into prison cells that they want so desperately to get out of. This volume can form the basis for discussions in many disciplines: philosophy, research, sociology, theology and many more. However, it is particularly aimed at African leaders at various levels, emerging academics in and outside their university auditoriums and common man/woman who can digest the conceptual ideas that are on offer and begin to engage with them as a viable alternative to the status quo. It would be disingenuous to argue that ideas discussed here are transposable. However, given the reflexivity that we humans are naturally endowed with, it is possible to imagine that *duality of structures* as interpreted here, *methodological dilemmas*, *de-contextualisation issues* and *duality of structures inspired leadership* of various fields such as DRC and Sub-Saharan universities would be of relevance to someone in a non-African setting.

A major challenge, in my view, is the argument of applying a theoretical concept plucked out of its European setting to an African one. I pre-empt such a criticism by devoting an entire chapter that discusses more widely the issue of (double) de-contextualisation.

However, it could be argued that de-contextualisation rhetoric is a discourse that is used by the African elites to position themselves as indispensable players in explaining, shaping and reshaping of African social reality. There is a growing unease reflected even in the academic world where, for decades, African studies as a discipline has had 'its primary motive and the logic that continues to propel it are aimed at decoding Africa and Africans for the world and not vice versa, still less the African world for African' (Olukoshi 2006:539). The lack of internal debate among Africans does only feed into popular scepticism towards African leaders, academics and yet another publication on Africa.

Scepticism from the masses (the agents who are supposed to shape and reshaped social reality), instead, is the biggest obstacle that this publication could face. Africa is not short of learned and well intentioned individuals (elites) whose actions once in positions of responsibility have not always matched their spoken and/or written words. While such cynicism/scepticism is justifiably legitimate, this publication is not intended to be an application for an inexistent job/role for the author but rather for the cynical and non-cynical alike to take up the agentic job of shaping and reshaping their social realities. If I had to summarise, on basis of the author's passion rather than self-publicity, this entire publication in one sentence, I would say: 'this is your handbook for truly African cultural, economic, journalistic, leadership, political, religious, research, etc., actions'.

Préface

Dans le chapitre intitulé '*Le mouvement vers la démocratie: perspectives mondiales, continentales et de l'Etat*', Wiseman (2002:2) fait la remarque suivante à propos du continent Africain : 'l'Afrique n'est pas un acteur majeur sur la scène mondiale. En terme militaire et économique, elle est extrêmement faible'. Dans cette publication '*L'Afrique à travers la Théorie de la Structuration - ntu*', l'auteur cherche à résoudre un problème persistant de la pauvreté - soit chronique et transitoire (Aliber 2003), sous-développement et déceptions dans le continent Africain. Cela se fait en attirant l'attention sur le leadership. Il me serait difficile d'exécuter un tel projet, sauf s'il était planté dans un contexte sociologique approprié. La théorie de la structuration d'Antony Giddens (1979; 1984), par conséquent, sert de tremplin à conceptualiser les divers faits historiques en ce qui concerne à la fois la structure et l'action. Par conséquent, l'auteur propose la dualité du structurel (la récursivité entre l'action et la structure) comme une solution aux problèmes actuels de leadership.

Il est important d'évoquer un bref récit juste pour nous rappeler de la nature du problème avant d'expliquer comment les questions spécifiques qui y sont abordées s'enchaînent. L'Afrique, à n'importe quel point de repère, peut être conçue comme un lieu géographique où la majorité de la population vit dans la pauvreté malgré toutes les ressources disponibles. Au cours des dernières années, il y a un air d'investissement renouvelé sur le continent. Mais, si ces efforts aboutissent, un tel succès viendrait sur les talons d'un passé désastreux. Le paradoxe de la 'pauvreté malgré la richesse' est commun. Par exemple dans *West Africa Hosts Untapped Mineral Wealth*, l'auteur anonyme (2010) décrit le Burkina Faso comme hébergeant :

> Une partie de la richesse géographique inexploitée dans le continent Africain. Mais en raison d'une histoire d'instabilité politique, coups d'Etat militaires, sécheresse extrême et de la législation défavorable à l'investissement, il n'est pas surprenant que, jusqu'à récemment, les grandes entreprises ont évité d'y investir (54).

À propos du Niger, il fait remarquer que 'le pays a souffert d'une histoire politique agitée et reste désespérément pauvre' (56) en dépit de son uranium et d'autres minerais tels que l'or. À propos de Liberia, l'auteur mentionne son minerai de fer:

> Les exportations de minerai de fer ont représenté plus de la moitié des recettes d'exportation totale du pays et c'est une source majeure d'emploi pour les locaux. Cette industrie de fer a été brusquement interrompue par la guerre civile et de combats continuels entre 1989 et 2003. La violence a laissé la nation déchirée par la guerre, paralysée et pauvre, même selon les normes Afrique de l'Ouest (57).

En ce qui concerne la Guinée-Conakry, l'auteur parle de 30% des réserves de bauxite du monde qu'abrite le pays avant de souligner ses minerais d'or et dépôts de fer. Malgré cette richesse et les dernières 'élections démocratiques' de 2010, la paix est encore précaire et le pays doit trouver une voie de sortie de la pauvreté qui en a résulté en partie par le régime autoritaire dans lequel il a été plongé juste après l'indépendance en 1958.

Sur le front de l'énergie, il reste encore beaucoup à faire. Alors que la population Africaine devrait croître de 71% en 2035, l'approvisionnement en énergie est attendu à 38% seulement. Ceci doit interpeller du fait que le continent Africain a

> En abondance, le gaz naturel et le pétrole dans le nord et l'ouest, le charbon en Afrique du sud, et des ressources en eau en Afrique centrale. L'Afrique peut être considérée comme un géant panneau solaire, et le vent est abondant dans le désert aride et les régions côtières. Il n'y a pas pénurie de ressources énergétiques, traditionnelles ou renouvelables (Naidoo et Bacela 2012:67-68).

Bien que la liste des échecs soit énorme, il ya certainement de quoi se réjouir. La lutte personnelle et institutionnelle contre l'apartheid de l'ancien président sud-africain Nelson Mandela se démarque comme l'un des exemples. Cependant, plus d'une décennie depuis que Wiseman (2002) a fait le commentaire utilisé pour commencer cette préface, les histoires de déception et des occasions ou opportunités manquées continuent à affliger le continent. 'Dans certains pays africains, le niveau de vie a diminué non seulement en terme relatif mais aussi en terme absolu' (Giddens 2002 : XXVII).

La situation est tellement désespérée qu'on se demande si l'Afrique est prédéterminée à vivre de cette manière comme un chien est prédéterminé à manger les os. Mais ici, chacun de nous doit se rappeler le proverbe Akan (Ghana et Côte d'Ivoire) qui dit 'les chiens ne préfèrent pas les os à la viande;

c'est juste qu'on ne leur donne jamais la viande'. Les soulèvements populaires des jeunes qui ont secoué la Tunisie, l'Egypte, le Burkina Faso, la République Démocratique du Congo (RDC) ... peuvent être considérés comme un spectacle de la détermination de l'Afrique à être reconnue comme une force démocratique et économique sur la scène mondiale, des moments où les chiens ont voulu réaménager le menu et échanger les os pour la viande.

Cette publication tente d'offrir une voie de sortie à travers une conceptualisation théorique rigoureuse qui identifie le leadership comme un problème en Afrique et offre des idées d'application de la théorie de la structuration de Giddens. Elle pourrait être considérée comme un exercice purement intellectuel, abstrait et idéaliste. En guise de réponse, il faudrait d'abord reconnaitre qu'en abordant les questions qui touchent à l'essence d'un peuple (les Africains en l'occurrence), la philosophie et l'abstraction s'imposent au lieu d'être une indulgence purement académique et stérile. Deuxièmement, cette publication est conçue comme un guide pratique qui utilise des exemples concrets et en effet, rallie l'abstraction à la réalité. Le style de leadership de Nelson Mandela pourrait être considéré comme un prototype de ce que l'auteur préconise, mais sa réalisation avec succès dans l'avenir dépendra évidemment de la volonté de tous les acteurs et toutes les structures qui sont assez honnêtes pour reconnaître les limites des anciennes pratiques et donner la chance à l'innovation.

Ce livre est donc une entreprise conceptuelle qui s'appuie sur des sources secondaires plutôt que des recherches de premier degré menées en Afrique. Il offre un (des) modèle (s) ou grille (s) analytique (s) pour conceptualiser les problèmes sociaux / défis actuels en Afrique, déclencher des réflexions et tirer des leçons de leadership (et d'autres concepts connexes) pour enfin renverser et inverser le récit actuel de pauvreté.

Par ailleurs, l'argument central ici est déductif et inductif. Cette publication met en évidence un argument déductif dans la mesure où elle commence à partir d'une théorie sociologique générale pour comprendre un contexte particulier notamment l'Afrique, même si l'idée d'un contexte africain homogène est quelque peu problématique.

En outre cette publication met de l'avant un argument inductif. Bien que les travaux de Kimoyo (2008), Smeulers et Hoex (2010) entre autres, que l'auteur utilise un peu plus tard, ne font pas des références explicites sur la théorie de la structuration mais, en réalité, les conclusions de ces études sont basées sur une oscillation entre l'action (les agents ou les citoyens) et la structure (les institutions gouvernementales et autres). On pourrait inférer des études de premier degré de Kimoyo et de Smeulers et Hoex une récursivité entre la structure et l'action. Avec l'intégration des exemples concrets des autres auteurs sur l'Afrique et ailleurs, ne pas considérer les conclusions de cet ouvrage '*l'Afrique à travers la Théorie de la Structuration – ntu*' comme basées sur une entreprise inductive est tout simplement une tentative arbitraire de subordination des sources secondaires à des sources primaires.

Quel que soit l'ordre d'importance que le lecteur attribue à des sources primaires ou secondaires, l'inclusion de ces exemples doit rassurer que cette publication n'est pas fondée sur des déclarations acceptées comme valables sans (preuve ou) être soumises à des tests sur leur validité (Dixon 1977 :119). Cela dit; Le livre est divisé comme suit:

Chapitre 1 '*African-Centred Leadership and the Theory of Structuration: a response to Obiakor*' présente une des façons suggérée par Obiakor (2004) pour résoudre le problème persistant de la pauvreté sur le continent africain. Il analyse les arguments qui y sont présentés et à l'aide de la théorie de la structuration, le chapitre se termine en suggérant une approche légèrement différente à adopter quant à la lutte contre le sort des Africains. La nouvelle perspective mérite d'être perçue pas comme une réaction à une approche différente, mais aussi comme une philosophie à part entière, d'où le deuxième chapitre qui sert de base à ce chapitre et la suite.

Chapitre 2 'Structure and agency dichotomy: an issue of trust?' fait la revue du débat entre la structure et l'action, apporte quelques exemples contemporains de l'Europe, mais surtout de l'Afrique, et démontre que la structure (les institutions) et l'action (les agents) ont brisé la confiance de l'une et de l'autre et qu'il nous faut la dualité du structurel pour restaurer la confiance brisée entre les deux.

Chapitre 3 'Duality of structures: a, not THE, methodology' examine les questions ontologiques, épistémologiques, éthiques et d'autres spécifiquement liées à l'Afrique. Dans le premier chapitre, l'auteur suggère que 'l'auto-examen en hausse' de la part des dirigeants et la 'peur en baisse' de la part de la population sont les deux indicateurs d'un exercice serein de la dualité du structurel pour restaurer la confiance brisée entre la structure et l'action. En réexaminant la conception Africaine de l'ontologie, l'épistémologie et de la méthodologie, l'auteur mène des analyses qui portent à suggérer un chevauchement entre la théorie de la structuration et l'ontologie Africaine (ntu). Mais si une telle analyse ne vous convainc pas en tant que lecteur, l'auteur reconnaît que c'est en partie due à une croyance enracinée qui traite 'd'étranger', du 'néo-colonialisme' et en effet inapproprié dans le contexte Africain tout ce qui, de loin ou de prêt, a trait à l'Occident. Ce point fait planer le doute sur le fond de cette publication qui effectivement utilise la théorie d'Antony Giddens (Britannique) sur le contexte africain. Le chapitre suivant en discute de façon détaillée.

Chapitre 4 *'Double de-contextualisation: a methodological myth or reality?'* s'engage avec les questions de de-contextualisation. La modernité est caractérisée par une mobilité accrue et des frontières floues. Et pourtant il faut se poser la question : quelles connaissances et intelligences appartiennent exclusivement à l'Afrique et non à l'occident et vice versa ? Il est donc essentiel qu'un répertoire des arguments soit développé pour justifier l'utilisation des idées autrement dites 'étrangères' sur le continent Africain. Il y a ici un élément de la liberté académique soutenu pas du point de vue des droits de l'homme, mais plutôt en faisant recours aux arguments scientifiques.

Le dernier chapitre *'Higher education in the DRC and Sub Saharan Africa: an example of duality of structures in action'* examine l'enseignement supérieur en RDC et en Afrique sub-saharienne. Contrairement au troisième chapitre dont la méthodologie éclaire la façon de mener des recherches basées sur la dualité du structurel, ce chapitre propose un cadre de conception de leadership et de programmes d'études universitaires en RDC et en Afrique subsaharienne. Il se veut un exemple pratique de la dualité du structurel. C'est seulement à cause de son expérience professionnelle et académique dans l'enscignement que l'auteur discute les 'universités' ici. Sinon, plusieurs autres exemples dans des domaines tels que la santé, la justice, la religion, les affaires et les médias dans différentes parties du continent pourraient être (ont été) étudiés. Il y a sans doute de telles initiatives déjà et beaucoup plus vont certainement continuer à traiter des questions spécifiques de réduction de la pauvreté à partir de diverses perspectives dans différents domaines. Cependant, ce que cette publication fait aussi est de souligner la nécessité d'un cadre conceptuel convergeant qui guiderait ces actions.

'Si vous voulez aller vite (*ou nulle part* - mes italiques), aller seul. Si vous voulez aller loin, aller ensemble' - proverbe africain. Cette sagesse africaine résume la pensée qui est proposée tout au long des chapitres précités, celle de la nécessité d'une interaction entre la structure et l'action.

Cette publication est destinée à tout le monde qui se soucis du sort des millions d'Africains dont les patries se sont transformées en cellules de prison. Elle s'adresse particulièrement aux dirigeants africains à tous les niveaux, des universitaires émergents dans et en dehors de leurs auditoires universitaires et hommes/femmes qui peuvent digérer les idées conceptuelles qui y sont proposées et commencer à s'engager avec eux comme une alternative viable au statu quo. Il serait malhonnête de prétendre que les idées discutées ici sont transposables. Cependant, compte tenu de la réflexivité dont nous sommes naturellement douées entant qu'êtres humains, il est possible d'imaginer que la dualité du structurel (*ntu*) telle qu'interprétée ici, les dilemmes méthodologiques, les questions de de-contextualisation et la dualité du structurel pour le leadership des universités en RDC et en Afrique subsaharienne inspireraient quelqu'un (e) dans un contexte non-africain.

Le défi majeur, à notre avis, est l'argument de l'application d'un concept théorique arraché de son contexte 'Européen' dans un contexte Africain. L'auteur devance une telle critique en consacrant tout un chapitre qui traite plus largement de la question de la (double) dé-contextualisation.

En revanche, la rhétorique de de-contextualisation pourrait être considérée comme un discours utilisé par les élites africaines pour se positionner comme des acteurs indispensables pouvant façonner et expliquer la réalité sociale africaine. Il ya un malaise croissant dans le monde universitaire où, pendant des décennies, les 'études africaines' en tant que discipline se sont assignées comme 'motif primaire de décoder l'Afrique et les Africains pour le monde et non l'inverse, encore moins le monde africain pour l'Afrique' (Olukoshi 2006 :539). L'absence de débat interne parmi les Africains nourrit le scepticisme populaire envers les dirigeants africains, des universitaires et encore une énième publication sur l'Afrique.

C'est plutôt le scepticisme des masses (les agents qui sont censés façonner et remodeler la réalité sociale), qui représente le plus grand obstacle au quel cette publication pourrait faire face. L'Afrique n'est pas à court d'individus compétents, bien intentionnés et éduqués dont les actions une fois dans les postes de responsabilité n'ont toujours pas reflétés leurs paroles et/ou écrits. Bien que tel cynisme/scepticisme soit légitime, cette publication n'est pas une demande d'emploi incxistant pour l'auteur, mais plutôt pour le cynique et non-cynique à s'engager dans l'action de modeler et remodeler leurs réalités sociales.

Chapter 1

'African-Centred leadership' and the theory of structuration: a response to Obiakor

Abstract:

Dissatisfaction with one system of organisation or governance can lead to calls for a change for the better. There are numerous such calls specifically aimed at Africa wanting, hoping and urging it to emerge and better the lives of its people. One suggestion that is represented here by accounts from the 2004 Obiakor's article has been for Africa to recapture itself in a typical Hegelian cycle of opposites of structures or systems of governance. This chapter attempts to reframe the problem with African leadership using Giddens' duality of structures and proposes a slightly different discourse that should be given voice in the African leadership narrative and renaissance.

Introduction

This chapter uses Giddens' (1979, 1984) social theory of *duality of structures* to reconceptualise the narrative of renewing with 'intrinsic' African values associated with the pre-colonial Africa, lost in the colonial era, and further alienated in the post-colonial time. It begins with a summary and then an analytical review of Obiakor's (2004) article which traces African leadership through the periods of pre-colonialism, colonialism, post-colonialism to post-dictatorship and advocates for an African-centred education that would

1

produce 'patriotic' leaders and ensure that Africa makes an irreversible entry into prosperity. The review is then followed by an outline of the theme of duality of structures within Giddens' social structuration theory which is linked to his views on modernity. His concepts equip my writing of this chapter with a theoretical framework to question and consider some of the pertinent issues that have so far remained unexamined. The section 'A new perspective for Africa using Giddens' structuration theory' re-examines the role that individual Africans would have played in the formation of their pre-colonial, colonial and post-colonial institutions. Reflecting on what needs to be done if the leadership of current and future institutions/movements/projects (states, African-centred education, African renaissance etc.) is to be successful, the chapter concludes by arguing that a cross-section or multi-fields engagement with social phenomena that is constructed through the interplay of structure and agency is what is needed.

Giddens did not develop a coherent methodological perspective for his structuration theory; hence, an *increasing sense of self-scrutiny* on the one hand and *decreasing fear* on the other hand are my experience-based indicators of the effects of such interplay and could serve as possible ways of testing the duality of structures in the context that is discussed here.

There is something that the reader needs to know before proceeding. This chapter was originally submitted for publication in an international peer review Journal. It was accepted initially and the comments from reviewers are presented below. It was then denied publication for the reasons that appear at the end of the chapter where the author shares his response before proceeding on to other chapters.

Reviewer(s)'Comments to Author:

Reviewer1: Comments to the Author: I say well done and congratulation for engaging in an innovative thinking to solve an enduring problem; and also for promoting integrative analysis of multiple perspectives. That's good scholarship. However, avoid using Eurocentric terms such as "tribal." Also, make sure that at least one (XXX) reference is included in the reference section.

Reviewer 2, Comments to the Author: This article deals with an important topic and is worthy of publication with a minor revision. The article needs a careful revision in order to improve its overall clarity and readability. There are mechanical issues and awkward expressions here and there. Two examples will suffice.

The following unclear sentence appears on page 2: "One such question is: 'what has been and should be the role of Africans as actors in previous systems (pre-colonial, colonial and post-colonial) and future ones (institutionalised African-centred education, African renaissance etc.,) being put forward?"

Then, on page 3, there is also a convoluted construction: "He cites the example of chiefs allowing their children to inherit their thrones which he contrasts with a servant being able to marry a King's daughter if he were hard working, to make the point of the pragmatism of African culture but at the same time briefly allude to the 'structure and/versus agency' theme when he asserts that Africans 'did everything for themselves and their communities.'"

Why Obiakor matters and what does he say? A summary

Social media and academic work are awash with Africans bemoaning colonisation and what is believed to be its modern day mutations through globalisations, international bodies, and Western academies. Mentan's (2015) work entitled *Unmasking Social Science Imperialism: globalization theory as a phase of academic colonialism* is just one such example. Convinced by such legitimate rhetoric, you and I can be forgiven for looking for inspirational practices of leadership, for example, closer to home. The chances of achieving such a noble quest become improbable when the reality on the ground is that of nationalistic oppression as Mentan (2009) documents in *Democratizing or Reconfiguring Predatory Autocracy? Myths and Realities in Africa Today.*

Disillusioned by current practices of our fellow Africans in power, a recurrent salvific suggestion has been to renew with African traditional values. But just how do we go about it, what do we hope to find and how do we adapt that new knowledge to the world today? These are just some of the questions that are yet to be adequately articulated. Obiakor's (2004) article '*Building patriotic African leadership through African-centred education*' makes a contribution worth our attention.

Obiakor sees Africa generally regressing in its education standards, economies and political leadership despite isolated success stories in a handful of situations (countries). This, according to the author, is due to the adoption of Euro-centred frameworks. Those frameworks are not clearly articulated. However, in an attempt to resolve the situation, the author begins by bringing to our attention the assumption that 'the kind of education the citizens receive reflects the kind of leaders it produces' (Ibid 415). He then goes on to recommend the revamping of Africa's educational systems that would 'incorporate African-centred problem solving, partnership building, and collaboration and consultation' (Ibid 416) as its building blocks. With a robust African-centred education hangs Africa's ability to change attitudes through its systems of beliefs and ideals.

The rest of the author's article is essentially a historical retracing of events which brings him to the conclusion that the African traditional values to be enshrined in the African centred-education existed in the 'precolonial Africa and were lost during the colonial and postcolonial periods' (Ibid 416). Those values, according to the Obiakor, resurfaced in the leadership of Nelson Mandela, Julius Nyerere, Nkwame Nkrumah.

As we engage in a critical review of Obiakor's article in the next section, it is important that the views on African values and their presence and/or absence through the eras of pre-colonial, colonial and post-colonial do not go unquestioned and hopefully reframe what has come to epitomise the African narrative. With the reality of contrived collegiality (Hargreaves 2003), just how are we to understand collaboration here? Who is to collaborate with whom and on what basis? These are important questions that need answering.

When paying tribute to Nelson Mandela, the American president said:

> ...we will not see the likes of Nelson Mandela again, so it falls to us, as best as we can, to follow the example that he set, to make decisions guided not by hate, never discount the difference that one person can make and

strive for a future worthy of sacrifice (Barak Obama 6/12/2013).

The above extract is carefully worded. It recognises the 'unrepeatable' uniqueness of these great African leaders in 'we will not see the likes of Nelson Mandela again...' To that extent, those leaders had special traits that set them apart from the rest of us. The extract, however, recognises that (African) leadership is an art that can be learnt and developed: '...it falls to us, as best as we can, to follow their example...'

But how did these great African leaders exercise their leadership aimed at shepherding their nations to their 'true African-ness'? Was it just a matter of excavating those lost traditional values and reinstating them in the Africa of today? Are African education systems ready for the African-centred education that Obiakor and many others are proposing? The contention here is that, there is something much more central that needs to be articulated and through which African education and other fields can be understood. 'Education (*like leadership and others*, my Italics), in the African traditional setting cannot (and indeed philosophically should not) be separated from life' (Reagan 2005:62).

This chapter and the entire publication for that matter is an attempt to understand African life, whether modern or traditional. But there is also a moral duty that requires of us to engage in creative thinking in order to reverse the continent's on-going plights. This chapter begins a kind of pedagogy of African leadership ideals using structuration theory and the author argues, in later chapters, for a rapprochement between structuration theory and African ontology (*ntu*).

Obiakor and the African-centred education for African-centred leadership: a review

Obiakor (2004) is just one in a growing list (Du Bois 1973; Foster 1997; Lomotey 1994; Murrell 2002; Rabaka 2003; Warfield-Coppock 1995 and Wilson 1992) of academics who focus their writings on African-centred education. Reference to Du Bois' (1973) definition of African education will be made. This is essential in as far as it is rooted in African continental origins and 'values'.

To say that Obiakor (2004) is not impressed with African leaders in the time of writing his article is an understatement. He uses his breadth of knowledge drawing from different sources to make his central point about the need for African education systems to be African-centred which would lead to the production of more patriotic leaders who would, in his view, do better for future generations. African-centred education is only a means to achieving the goal of patriotic African leadership. The intention here is not to unpack the ins and outs of what he proposes as African-centred education; this chapter focuses instead on, as implied in his article, the ups and downs of his goal: 'African leadership'.

'The institutionalisation of a pragmatic system of African-centred education that opens concrete rooms for African experiments and African experiences and fosters the use of African body, soul and mind' (404) is an ideal that Obiakor (2004) traces back to the pre-colonial Africa. At that time, he argues, there was a pervasive sense of collaboration, trust, integrity, consensus, and amicable conflict resolution to name but just a few. Looking beyond single practices such as storytelling, the entire individual acts of pragmatism were, it would seem manifestations of what he calls the 'cultural continuity'. He cites the example of chiefs allowing their children to inherit their thrones which only highlights the 'passive' role that Africans would have played in the shaping of their institutions. One could argue that this may not have mattered to the '*Ubuntu*' style of leadership (Mbigi 1997) which is generous, people-oriented and as Obiakor (2004:407) would put it 'tied to the apron string of traditional African culture'.

To apply the same logic today does matter, not least because of the numerous acts of unpatriotic leadership throughout Africa. The degree of what Letseke (2013:351) calls 'shocking and horrifying incidents of moral indiscretions' (violent crime, premeditated murder, rape, assault, homophobic attacks and police brutality) in South Africa, which could be extended to the rest of the continent, is a reminder that Africans can be active agents (albeit in a negative way as implied in Letseke's article) and, more importantly, that healthier articulations/expressions/manifestations of *Ubuntu* and African-centred leadership are necessary. It suffices to say that the narrative of the pre-colonial Africa in Obiakor's article firmly grounds or subsumes the individual within the community and the temporal within the continuity. Individuals did not only act for themselves, they did so for the community since they are an extension of the whole, of the structure.

The good times, or better still the seamless flow of the 'cultural continuity', seemed to have been interrupted by what he calls the 'Eurocentric intrusion' which according to Onwudiwe and Ibelema (2003) continues to be felt today though not known now as 'colonisation' as it was then. This intrusion is presented by Obiakor as another system that

8

superseded African cultural continuity. This system, on which the author only focuses his critique on education, is characterised as leading to the satisfaction of European selfish ends, and destroying traditional African values and their gatekeepers (resisting rulers and chiefs) on its expansion pathway. In what seems to be the continuation of his theme of Africans as individual moral and reflexive actors being lost in the changing structures, Obiakor cites the example of traditional courts replacing the African family collaborative structures in resolving problems. The mushroom courts were representative of a version of structures/systems that did not tolerate any deviant individual acts. Another structure or institution that is cited is Christianity which 'destroyed some great traditional values' (408). Once again, the individual (African leader in this case), wherever he/she stood, was absorbed by the institution in such a way that he or she became a puppet serving the interests of the new (colonial) structure.

The advent of an independent Africa, according to the author, saw some examples of impressive leadership, but generally, the promises of self-determination were short lived. For the best cases of post-colonial Africa, the author cites the examples from Nigeria, Sudan and Tanzania for their daring authentic educational initiatives. The author does not state the goals in question but singles out Nigeria and Sudan as two of the nations that attempted to establish an education system with 'a national philosophy' (410). He then praises the patriotic move in Tanzania for its socialism agenda whose ideology 'transcended virtually all social, cultural, economic, educational, and political levels of Tanzania' (410). While others might see these changes as Marxist experiments with Soviet backing, it does not mean that they are un-African.

One can then say that these initiatives were nationalistic and to some extent still had an institutional dimension. However, Obiakor presents them as singular and conscious attempts to write one's own destiny rather than be part of a narrative that sees individual actions predetermined by a constraining (foreign) system. That, however, is still what happened according to Obiakor as colonial domination was replaced by African forms of (military) domination. The egoism of one tyrant meant that entire nations and all their subjects had to dance to the tunes of the new version of domination and, like in the colonial period, the deviants were decimated. Adi Amin's oppressive rule in Uganda and that of Mobutu in the then Zaire, are just two poignant examples to illustrate a new devastating episode in the chain succession of subjects' subsuming structures.

In summary then, the narrative of the African leader and Africans as subjects that Obiakor eloquently and patriotically presents can be understood as one string of structures after structures that have at times, especially in the pre-colonial Africa, encapsulated the African spirit and at other times, in this case the colonial and post-colonial, betrayed it. His optimistic post-dictatorial/military Africa is, in my reading of his argument, yet another indulgent moment with the structure of the pre-colonial Africa. The foregoing phrasing of Obiakor's narrative should not be misunderstood to be an anti-thesis to the consensus around the nobleness that the pre-colonial values represent. Most of them, for example: the freedom bells, fighting corruption, democracy, self-reliance and skills-focused education for problem solving, partnership building, collaboration and consultation are based, it would seem, on the principle of human justice and in a sense are not exclusive to Africa.

The *Pedagogy of the oppressed* by Freire (1970), for example, can be understood as a Latin American version of a call for more patriotic leaders who would put social justice at the heart of their policies. Underpinning the pre-colonial values, one could argue, is the desire to humanise. On the subject of humanisation, Freire (1970:25) writes 'both humanisation and dehumanisation are real alternatives, only the first is the people's vocation'. Yes, this vocation can be culturally ring fenced and protected but it is, according to Freire, a vocation of *the people*, which the author takes to mean *all* people. Humanity belongs to all and it could be argued that all the conceptual ideas (Giddens' and others that are highlighted in this chapter) that help 'humanise' different groups, irrespective of their cultural backgrounds, survive the bias of being another form of educational or intellectual neo-colonialism (Altbach 1971). To return to the main point, Obiakor's pursuit of a (pre-colonial) structural rediscovery leads him to argue that:

> '...Interestingly, these skills used to be evident during the pre-colonial Africa and were lost during the colonial and post-colonial periods' (416).

Writing in 2001, the then South African President Thabo Mbeki goes at great length to define the African renaissance by attempting to strike a balance between a return to a pre-colonial structure and at the same time redefine its very self. Addressing his South African audience, he says 'the institution of traditional leadership can and should play a central role in the African renaissance' and goes on to say '...to speak of African renaissance is to speak of coming into being of a new African identity...' Justifying this rhetoric was the setting up of an 'African recovery programme' by African leaders to eradicate poverty across the continent. It is worth noting that despite this initiative coming earlier than the writing of his article; it did not stop Obiakor (2004) from deploring what he saw as 'unpatriotic' leadership. Nevertheless, while Obiakor's African-centred education is a different initiative from the African recovery program of Mbeki in that the first produces great patriotic leaders and the second is a step towards the renewal of the new identity, they are both articulations of institutionalised vehicles for structural values to be transmitted. More efforts then need to be made to understand, define and promote the interactions that individual subjects or citizens have had with previous structures and will have with the new suggested structures. Simply appealing to people to create and commit to new structures that supposedly have people's interests at heart (be it African-centred education or African recovery programs), without giving voice to an agentic African narrative seems to me short of a credible renaissance and (African-centred) leadership.

For the purpose of my argument, the next section outlines Giddens' (1979) theory of structuration and appreciates its relevance in the context of a more globalised world or high modernity (Giddens 1984). This leads to posing some pertinent questions regarding the place of African citizens in what the author deems to be a one-sided structuration narrative. The section refers to Giddens' original texts as well as other commentaries (Archer 1995; Elster 1982; Fuchs 2003; Jones and Karsten 2008; and Stones 2005) that faithfully elucidate on and scrutinise his rather complex theory.

Giddens' theory of structuration

Giddens (1979), like Bourdieu (1984) for example, is concerned with the dichotomisation of structure and human agency in the shaping of social reality. He dislikes functionalism which places the system needs over and above the needs of individuals. Giddens' call to social theorists then, and the author would argue that the same call applies to those attempting to understand social phenomena with an economic, political, cultural and ethical interest, is to bear in mind that,

> The pressing task facing social theory today is not to further the conceptual elimination of the subject, but on the contrary, to promote a *recovery of the subject* without lapsing into subjectivism. Such a recovery, I wish to argue involves a grasp of what cannot be said (or thought) as *practice* (Giddens 1979:44).

In an attempt to provide a coherent social theory that is not caught up in the logic of either functionalism or interpretism, either structure or agency, Giddens proposes that social environment be viewed in a *duality of structures.* This concept is essential in understanding the interplay that Giddens envisages between structure and agency and therefore avoid the imperialism of the subject advocated by the interpretive sociologists against that of the social order vehemently defended by the functionalists/structuralists (Fuchs 2003). He first sees societies as having rules and resources. The duality of such structural properties is felt in that they both constrain and enable. One of the succinct ways of explaining the constraining and enabling process of social phenomena is by Jones and Karsten (2008). They argue that,

> Giddens proposes that structure and agency are a mutually constitutive duality. Thus social phenomena are not the product of *either* structure *or* agency, but of both. Social structure is not independent of agency, nor is agency independent of structure. Rather, human agents draw on social structures in their actions, and at the same time these actions serve to produce and reproduce social structure (129).

In this way of thinking, there is room to argue that the past could have been (and the future could be) different, as structures get reproduced through the instantaneous actions of individuals. This dialectic between agency and structure and its focus on the here and now has come under criticism. The first is not so much of a criticism as Giddens is aware of the fact that the natural world has a constraining hold on individuals without giving the actors any enabling option. To illustrate this, one has only got to imagine that one cannot walk across the Atlantic Ocean without drowning. Metaphorically and in the context of the social world then, pre-existent social actions (Archer 1995) can define the conditions within which one acts in the present. These pre-existent social actions (elected or imposed as laws and norms) are, according to Stones (2005), what Archer refers to as external structures and Giddens calls the objective existent. They both refer to structural properties that the individual cannot change.

To further clarify structuration theory, Stones (2005:20) argues that the pre-existent social actions or norms are not to be thought of in a causal process where there is a 'sequence in terms of a discrete structural moment being succeeded by a discrete and entirely separate moment of agency, which is then succeeded by another discrete moment of structure, and so on'. With regard to the ability of individual agents to change their environment in the on-going dialectic of duality of structures, Giddens distinguishes between the constraint as normative sanction and as structural constraint (Stones 2005). In the former, rules and norms may build pre-existent conditions that are resistant to change. However they, especially inequitable rules, 'are not experienced that way as they don't prevent her from doing what she wants to do – they may even enable, facilitate desired actions' (Stones 2005: 59) though gatekeepers of the structure may impose punishment on the transgressors. A bit like some aspects of the natural world that cannot be changed (the example of 'not being able to walk across the Atlantic ocean without drowning' has been used here while Giddens uses the example of 'a person not being able to walk through a wall'), the latter, structural constraints, refers to engagement, contract or even norms that confront the actor as an external reality which cannot be changed, but that is only in as far as it is viewed as an external reality. It is worth wondering whether, in social interactions, constraints as normative sanction are ascribed the same nature as structural constraints and vice versa.

To summarise the argument, Giddens' structuration theme of duality of structures has highlighted a number of things. The first is the primacy of the duality of structures over dualism. This means that social phenomena are no longer to be regarded as an exclusive domain of either objective social structures or the individual subjects. Ontologically, objective social structures and individuals are now to be regarded as standing on equal footing. Historically, the past, present and future are a mobilisation of structural resources by individuals who, in turn, reproduce structures. To elucidate on this point, Stones (2005:21) writes,

> the structures, in a sense, must come first into the agents before they can be drawn upon. Agents have structures within them. Equally, structures – the perceived configurations of legitimate and illegitimate actions, conventionally accepted meanings, and distributions of economic and authoritative power – are seen both to have agents within them and to be the product of agents.

The recognition of individuals' agency is even more essential as traditional structures, that would have guided individual actions, dissolve as a result of globalisation and modernity through increased information technology. Skilled social actors that would reflexively shape and reshape the new institutions in the context of what Giddens (1984) calls 'high modernity' are necessary.

Secondly, both Obiakor and the author write with a social justice agenda, which is to emancipate and make human life more liveable. A value free historical interplay between social structures and individual agents, therefore, is not enough. Hence, the resources that constitute the social structures are both individuals' *responsibility* and an *opportunity*. A responsibility in that they (individuals) would have contributed to its existence and an opportunity since the resources can still be used dialectically to reproduce further structures and change the course of history for the better.

There are rules that can constrain but it is important to remind ourselves that unlike the natural world that cannot be changed, we agree to engage with constraint as normative sanction not because the social world imposes unchangeable structural constraints on us. The rules and norms as normative sanctions can enable and facilitate desired actions (Stones 2005:9).

There can also be a tendency when thinking about these concepts to conceptualise the interaction between structure and agency as an end in itself. The responsibility and opportunity element root the theory of duality of structures firmly on the central goal of critical theory which is human emancipation (Britannica academic edition). The next section uses Giddens' concept of duality of structures to reframe the African-centred education or African leadership discourse.

A new perspective for Africa using Giddens' structuration theory

It is now worth looking back before looking forward. Before attempting to outline a new approach in the African leadership narrative in the light of Giddens' structuration theory, it is essential that a retrospective reflection that would affirm the centrality of the theme of duality of structures in the African leadership narrative is provided.

One area of reflection is what appears to be the tyranny of various structures over individual emancipatory prospects. The historical turning points, right from the pre-colonial to the 'post-dictatorial/military' Africa, appear to be the time when structures were the way through which to conceptualise individuals. In the pre-colonial time, individuals were at an advantage which they lost in the colonial and dictatorial eras. The thinking seems to have been dominated by a tendency to replace what seems dysfunctional in the eyes of colonial Europeans with regard to pre-colonial values and post-colonial 'unpatriotic' (to stick to Obiakor's terms) leaders with regard to colonial values with another structure. It is therefore legitimate to wonder if Africa is effectively in an endless cycle of recreating the problems that she was dissatisfied with in the first place.

The view here is that it is possible to recreate earlier problems if no attempt is made to reframe the problems that the African continent has encountered thus far. As indicated above, the problem does not lie in a bad system superseding a good one but rather in failing to recognise the role that individuals have played and need to play by drawing on the structural resources to produce and reproduce their social structures (Giddens 1979). Below are a few examples to illustrate this point.

A pre-colonial example

Though one of Fafunwa's (1975, 1976) goals for education in the pre-colonial time, as cited by Obiakor (2004:406), was to 'inculcate respect for elders and those in position of authority', this could not be possible if individual acts by Africans did not happen to produce what is referred to, nostalgically, as 'African values'. When placed in space and time, these values (or structural resources to use Giddens' terms) were produced by agents of that time and there is no guarantee that agents interacting with structures today would reproduce the same values as those of the pre-colonial era unless one decides to defend a philosophy contrary to the one implied in Heraclitus' famous metaphor which reads *one cannot step in the same river twice* (Johnson 2004). Hence, the African traditional values were what they were because individual agents made the structures what they were then. 'No traditional societies were wholly traditional, and traditions and cultures have been invented for diversity of reasons' (Giddens 2002:40). Let us use an abridged version of one of African stories (from *'Keeping the Promise'* - unpublished) as an illustration.

Desperate to raise a child of their own, a couple goes to see a witch doctor to help the wife conceive. The witchdoctor performs his magic and next the lady falls pregnant. Rather than conceiving a baby, she carries a monster instead. Sensing some strange things in the house, the husband is instructed by another with doctor to exorcise the wife and the monster leaves finally her.

The moral, and arguably at the heart of African value system, is the idea that children are a God given gift other than it being the domain of witchdoctors. We may seek to inculcate this African and also ecumenical value to the next generations. But the development of modern technological procedures such as IVF that Africans may (or may not) want to use, for example, make a reframing of the whole narrative an essential enterprise.

The focus, therefore, should not be on 'African values *per se*' but rather on better and healthier interactions between Africans and institutions that they help to create. In community cultures 'where a singular feeling (*reasoning or choosing* – my italics) self is not necessarily the primary axis of signification (Riessman 2008:2), highlighting the role of individuals may seem an unsettling proposition. Such a constituency need not worry since my argument, in the light of Giddens' theory, is not about a lapsing into subjectivism but rather making subjects take their effective role in the building (producing and reproducing) of social and communal structures. In societies that take pride in their traditions, 'becoming detraditionalised' (Giddens 2002:43) does threaten many things, not least people's identities. The agenda of duality of structures as used here is not an attempt to erode and replace traditions but rather to renew, rethink and get to grips, as it were, with the real African values and traditions in order to guide actions for a better Africa. It is therefore inaccurate to consider African values without recognising the contribution of everyone albeit within the rules and resources available to them at any given time, the pre-colonial in this case.

A colonial example

As already said, this period was characterised by 'Eurocentric intrusion'. It had 'puppet' leaders. The term 'puppet' can be taken to mean brainwashed people who are trained to think and act as they are told without having a mind of their own. However, since the vast majority of Africans then had a mind of their own, it is logically sound and within the theory of structuration to argue that puppets acted in accordance with the norms which they could not change for fear of sanctions. Such constraints, in Giddens' term, are constraints as a normative sanction and did not prevent individual agents from doing what they wanted to do even to the point of going against what one had to do. Inexcusable acts of cruelty of the colonial era will remain what they are and were and the thinking here is not that of victimisation. It is, rather, recognising the pivotal role that subjects play in the reproduction of societies and begin to

20

realise that new structures that suppress individuals are based on shaky grounds.

A post-colonial or independence example

After citing the example of Idi Amin's unpatriotic rule in Uganda, Obiakor concludes by saying 'it might be reasonable to summarise that, during postcolonial period, education failed to emancipate the African people' (2004:412). What suffered, in my view, were not the African values that, as already argued, would not be the same today even if the colonial era had not been there. It was rather the place/role of the individual in the shaping of a society in which he or she was a proud agent.

It has been said earlier that the aim here is not to unpack what 'African-centred education' might mean. However, it is worth mentioning that the idea of education being used to determine the path that individuals would take instead of promoting and empowering individuals to reshape their social structures is rather contentious. Those who might want to develop Obiakor's idea of 'African-centred education', would then be faced with the task of clarifying where it sits in the continuum of 'education for the economic needs of a nation' on the one hand and 'education for its own sake/development of subjective thinking skills' on the other hand (Hodge 2012), or integrate both principles. An elaboration of the concept of 'African-centred education' is even more necessary so that it does not become a perpetuation of specific power relations that favour the dominant societal classes (Bourdieu and Passeron 1990; Grenfell 2008) as the pre-colonial example mentioned earlier might suggest.

Du Bois (1973), for example, has advanced a theory of African education that could help to avoid the perpetuation of dominant classes. His work is primarily aimed at the education of African Americans in the United States. However, his theory of education is linked to the historical and geographical origins of African Americans which, in my view, makes it somewhat applicable to Africa as a continent. African education is defined as involving a critical study of African as well as world history, critical cultural study and an understanding of present and future vital needs of not only continental and diasporan Africans but also of humanity as a whole (Du Bois 1973). Such a view of African education cannot flourish if structural and institutional values of the pre-colonial era, for example, are all that we are concerned with. The critical approach advocated by Du Bois suggests that a different understanding of the unfolding of social phenomena is necessary. That it is not bounded but rather dynamic, interactive and globalised which requires skilled social actors to shape and reshape modern (not idealised traditional African) institutions (Giddens 1984). It is the contention here therefore that validating 'African-centred education' can be considered only as an attempt to make a more serious point about reviving or recovering a healthy agentic force that would rehabilitate societal structures.

Even when assuming that the argument that has been made so far can stand the scrutiny of its harshest critics, there is yet an unresolved question of, how in African contexts, one can concretely operationalize and get a feel of a duality of structures' inspired leadership. In general terms, its best concrete application would be felt when individuals and societies interpret and act on their social realities in a way that alienates neither one nor the other. There are, however, some small steps that can be taken that are discussed below.

Looking ahead: taking small concrete steps

An essentialist approach to African-centred education would characterise it as being able to alter the deep-rooted disposition of an individual that would make him or her act patriotically in a position of leadership. What this does is exclude the vast majority of people who fall outside of the affordability-based education and sideline them from playing an active role in the duality-of-structures based construction of social phenomena. In addition to this is the question of whether formal education is a liminal stage where new ideas about society get created or a reflection of the unfolding social life (Hargreaves 2003). The position here is that, it is both. And in as far as it is a reflection of social life; formal education is only one of the many theatres, or fields' to use Bourdieu's (1993) term, of the duality of structures. A non-exhaustive list of other theatres could be hospitals, religious groups, associations, cultural groups, the media, governments, regional and international bodies. To bring all these fields into play, a cross-section engagement with social phenomena that is constructed through the interplay of structure and agency is what is needed. And it cannot happen unless it is triggered by, whether lobbied and willing or pressurised, leaders of all these theatres. This, somewhat civil society tone may have Eurocentric origin but it is also what would have characterised the vision of arguably great patriotic African leaders such as Nelson Mandela.

From the author's experience of growing up in, visiting some other central African countries and receiving a Western higher education, one is able to propose some perhaps early indicators or signs of a healthier engagement with the duality of structures. They are *increasing self-scrutiny* by those in leadership positions accompanied with *decreasing fear* on the part of individuals. In an environment where politics is a dirty word and associated with dishonesty, *increasing self-scrutiny* has to be done with *honesty*. And yet, it is almost impossible to penetrate the realm of 'people's intentions' for us to tell with precision if they are being honest or not. *Decreasing fear* on the part of individuals then becomes the only reliable measurement of sincere increased self-scrutinising structures. These two elements are what should theoretically be the guiding force of not only the many national conferences, dialogues or other variations *'les concertations nationales'* as well as truth and reconciliation commissions but also of the business of leading public institutions.

Some literature on truth and reconciliation commissions, for example, have focussed on whether truth does actually lead to reconciliation (Gibson 2004). If 'truth' is not a given, then it might be procedurally worthwhile to invest some of our research energy into understanding whether structures allow (self) scrutiny and that subjects would feel free enough to tell the truth that would shape and reshape their institutions (example: a more reconciled society). What has been missing in African literature therefore is empirical research based on the degree to which individuals have felt a sense of agency in shaping and reshaping their social structures.

How do the two indicators apply in the leadership of Nelson Mandela held here as a prototype of structuration theory-*ntu*? There are many examples of his leadership where *increasing self-scrutiny* on the part of an institution lead to *decreasing fear* on the part of the South Africans in a compressed time and space and we hope that other writers, even posthumous biographers, will begin to enlighten the world with more examples of Mandela's leadership of institutional *increased self-scrutiny* and citizens' *decreasing fear*. We will however provide two that happen in a decompressed time and space, meaning there is a distance in time and space between the two examples that are evoked here.

Under Mandela's leadership, Archbishop Desmond Tutu oversaw the proceedings of the truth and reconciliation commission which was an eloquent example of institutional *increased self-scrutiny*. This was not just about the past institutions coming clean about the atrocities under committed in their era but also a statement that leadership draws its strength from admitting its failure unreservedly and allowing the citizens to have a say on the shaping of the institutions of the future.

Despite retiring from active institutional politics, Mandela's leadership continued, this time drawing more attention to the promotion of agents' (Africans') *decreasing fear*. As the founder or co-founder of a group called 'the elders', a body that brings together older state's personalities around the world, Mandela presented this body as one whose aim was 'to support courage where there is fear, foster agreement where there is conflict and inspire hope where there is despair' (Mandela 2007). From our grasp and analysis of the current state of play in Africa, it does not take a genius to conclude that those living in fear and therefore in need of the support that Mandela was talking about are the agents, the citizens.

Giddens' failure to develop a coherent epistemology and methodology to go with his ontological concepts (Stones 2005) does not help. But that does not diminish the relevance of his conceptual thinking that this chapter hopes to have been able to demonstrate as well as engage with the challenge of identifying a suitable epistemology when debating similar ideas in similar contexts. Hence researching people's sense of (decreasing) fear and their ability to (self) scrutinise institutions and societal structures become potential indicators of Giddens' duality of structures.

However, the prospects of whether possible 'truth and reconciliation commissions' or national conferences or dialogues or 'concertations' run in the true spirit of Giddens' structuration theory are slim if this miniature duality of structures is not replicated in the day-to-day affairs of, say, any governing activities. This is where my growing concern with information ministries on the African continent comes in. These government institutions feel more like internal or external self-defence and propaganda mechanisms instead of being used as means for self-scrutiny for internal efficacy and citizens' opportunity to shape and reshape their structures. Decreasing self-scrutiny in brutal regimes of post-colonial Africa does not help decrease but it rather increases fear amongst individual agents and perhaps makes constraints as normative sanctions seem like structural constraints.

Conclusion

An analysis of Obiakor's (2004) synopsis of African eras from pre- to post-colonial Africa has led me to argue that the narrative so far has been essentially about a succession of different systems or structures of leadership which brings structure and agency dualism to the fore. With an interest in both understanding the role of Africans as actors in previous systems (pre-colonial, colonial and post-colonial) and redefining their place in current and future structures (states, institutionalised African-centred education, African renaissance etc.) being put forward, a much more focused analysis using Giddens' theme of duality of structures within his structuration theory has enabled me to propose a different reading of African history. This reading locates the ups and downs of African leadership in the use or neglect of individuals' agentic force to shape and reshape their social and political structures which need skilled social actors to keep up with continuous changes associated with the modern world. Challenging the essentialist view of education as a means to produce patriotic leaders, this chapter proposes a cross-section engagement of structure and agency with *increasing self-scrutiny* on the part of leaders and *decreasing fear* on the part of individual citizens as methodological indicators.

After the minor revisions, the article was denied publication, for the following reasons:

Comments to the Author: Reviewer 1

Who is Obiakor? Why is he important? What did he say that is worth listening to? There should be a summary of his main points before proceeding; otherwise, the article and its significance remain confusing.

The categories of "pre-colonial," "colonial," and "post-colonial" are very Eurocentric and need to be interrogated, especially in a paper dealing with "African-centeredness." By the way, why is not "African-centered" defined? What does it mean to the author?

There are too many "I" in this text, which gives the impression that the article is based more on opinion than research.

Why not use a theory produced by an Afrocentric theorist, like Molefi Asante, instead of one produced by Giddens, who certainly did not African in mind. This article reads as a purely intellectual exercise. It would benefit greatly from engaging truly Afrocentric scholarship and building upon it with an eye on making concrete recommendations on how to improve our reality.

Reviewer: 2 Comments to the Author

Scholars of the same intellectual persuasion as the author of "African-Centred Leadership and the Theory of Structuration" are likely to reason that this article makes a compelling case for a re-orientation and Africanization of the values that underlie African education in order to yield a set of leaders who would lead with a sense of patriotism. However, the paper seems to be weak on how this sort of almost revolutionary educational objective could be operationalized at the various levels of education in light of the well-entrenched and prevailing neo-colonial social orders on the continent. Perhaps, a discussion of the latter issue of "how" may become the subject of a sequel to this initial piece.

In response and to set the scene for subsequent chapters of this book, the author writes:

Dear Dr XXX,

I am grateful for the comments from the reviewers but I cannot hide my disappointment with the decision to deny publication of my article despite the glowing comments when it was initially accepted for publication. All I wanted was to share my thoughts on the matter and certainly was not intending to have the last word.

My paper devotes an entire section on Obiakor and his article published in (the X journal) with the same headings as "pre-colonial," "colonial," and "post-colonial". I adore the work of Molefi Asante but I simply wanted to introduce another way of thinking using Giddens. I didn't set out to carry out field work but argue a point using a specific theory and in that sense it is an intellectual work with a practical contribution, I hoped.

But I now understand that this may have something to do with (me) being of a particular intellectual persuasion as reviewer 2 seems to suggest. The second reviewer goes on to say that 'Perhaps, a discussion of the latter issue of "how" (this sort of almost revolutionary educational objective could be operationalized at the various levels of education in light of the well-entrenched and prevailing neo-colonial social orders on the continent) may become the subject of a sequel to this initial piece.

With these reviews in mind, it is evident that this chapter offers something worth considering especially in a world where solving problems requires freeing ourselves from a monolithic thinking of a zero-sum game called 'truly Afrocentric Scholarship' and embracing multiple perspectives as reviewer 1 seems to suggest. The first of the last two reviewers even misses the point when he or she asks why 'African-centred' is not defined. Yet what the entire chapter does is to define 'African-centred along the lines of the theory of structuration where the construction of social phenomenon is based on the interplay between structure and agency.

It is also true, as suggested by one of the reviewers, that this initial piece sets the ball rolling for a sequel, not only to address the 'how' question (methodology) but also to discuss other issues for example 'Why not use a theory produced by an Afrocentric theorist, like Molefi Asante, instead of one produced by Giddens, who certainly did not African in mind' picked up by the reviewers. Overall, this chapter can be viewed as reactionary in the sense that it is mainly a response to an article. Therefore, before other discussions are introduced, it is important to develop and apply *duality of structures* as an independent theoretical framework when talking about Africa. The following chapter attempts to do just that.

Acknowledgement: I am grateful to Dr Paul Garland for his critical readership and proofreading an earlier version of this chapter.

Chapter 2

Structure and agency: (an issue of trust?)

Abstract

Structure and agency have been, and perhaps continue to be, held at opposing ends of the argument about the nature of social phenomena. Individually, they can be said to refer to clear entities and are value laden. This chapter argues that the claim for primacy of one over the other can be said to revolve around the issue of trust that each of them assumes and assures the other. That sort of approach only stands if the trust narratives of both structure and agency were faultless. With stories of broken trust drawn mainly from the African continent, a case is made for Giddens' duality of structures being the basis for a credible way to restore trust and get structure and agency working together.

Introduction

In *Realist Social Theory: The Morphogenetic Approach* (1995), Archer mounts a sustained and perhaps a compelling critique of Giddens' duality of structures within his theory of structuration (Giddens 1979, 1984). One of the criticisms, that is repeated by Stones (2005:52) is the idea that structure and agency 'are mixed together and confused such that any analytical value possessed by the concepts in the first place disappears'. This chapter explores some analytical values that the concepts represent when thought about separately. It also highlights the role that both structure and agency have played

31

in diminishing their credibility vis-à-vis each other, hence the idea of 'crisis of trust' that appear later in this chapter. In the changing economic, environmental, social, educational, and political climate, the thinking is pushed further to focus on the value, not the alleged confusion, which could be borne out of the very fact of mixing the two concepts.

Structure

The concept of 'structure' has been at the heart of ideological schools of thought such as functionalism, structural functionalism, structuralism and post-structuralism. The aim here is neither to engage in systematic historical development of the concept as articulated by Saussure, Lévi-Strauss, Derrida, Wittgenstein, etc., nor to provide a straightforward and simple explanation of such an elusive concept (Sewell 1992). However unpalatable versions of 'structure' there may be, it is necessary to revisit certain reifications of the term in order to provide at least a basic introduction of what the concept 'structure' signifies. In this respect, it might be easier to conceptualise 'structure' as hard, material, patterning mechanism that has a life of its own and governs a series of other transient and individual happenings. It is the immutable stability that does not only transcend all but also within which everything fits. Whether that is a radicalised or basic version of functionalism or structuralism, it at least provides us with a starting point to begin identifying and naming various structures within everyday life. Borrowing from Durkheim's idea of *social facts* (1952), society within which individuals are members, culture as 'a pattern of basic assumptions that a given group has invented, discovered, or developed...' (Schein 1984:6), and language can be viewed as structural entities.

Structuralism has its critics. Saussure's theory of language, for example, overturns the thinking that there is structure especially in language and is reported to have concluded that 'there is no natural or necessary connection between words (signifiers) and the concepts of the things to which they refer (that which is signified). Their relationship is arbitrary' (Hatch and Cunliffe 2013:41)

Giddens, however, has identified some values that the concept of 'structure' has brought. A more extensive discussion of these benefits of structuralism can be found in *Central Problems in Social Theory* (Giddens 1974). Intending to make a different kind of argument (the bracketed part of the title of this chapter *'an issue of trust?'*), this chapter will outline those advantages without much emphasis on their limitations that Giddens was keen to point out in order to make the case for his theory of *duality of structure*. For Giddens then, the structuralism as a movement has made some significant contributions. When looking at the historicity of structuralist thinking, there is recognition of a temporal dimension within structuration. It represents the foundation of the theory of social reproduction which links to the recursive properties that the structures or 'virtual systems' have come to be. There is an attempt to de-centre the subject as well as to transcend object/subject dualism which Giddens cautions must be effectively done in a duality of structures. The final contribution that Giddens identifies is the analysis of the value of cultural objects. The view that nation states can be counted as cultural objects and the structural value it brings about is illustrated below.

Before we do that, it is important to remind ourselves of the social stabilising power that structure had in African (traditional) society. Contrary to what some Western scholars would say, Udokang (2014) traces the stability, order and harmony that African communal life had on the lives of the individuals. The author uses two quotations to highlight the benefit of structure in African traditional societies:

> There exist many laws, customs, set forms of behaviour, regulations, rules, observances and taboos constituting the moral code and ethics of a given community or society. Any breach of this code of behaviour is considered evil, wrong or bad, for it is an injury or destruction to the accepted social order and peace... (Mbiti 1969:205)

Breaches were not only considered bad, they were severely punished as the following quote shows

> Africans have traditionally been very conscious of the social dimension of morality. Morality is always seen in the social context. Hence any serious violation of the moral order has a social aspect which involves serious social consequences. The whole society is affected, for every evil act is an anti-social act which has adverse effects on the whole community (Tempels 1959:45).

By the end of colonialism and the wave of independence across the African continent in the 1960's (Thomson 2004), the independent states and their subsequent governments would have been (and arguably are still being) held as cultural objects for various individuals. Alluding to Anderson's (1991) idea of 'imagined communities', Thomson (2004) goes on to make a point that underpins the argument here about states, nations or more precisely African nationalism after independence being cultural objects with a structural significance. He sums the structural mood with the following:

> Using interpretations of the past and symbols such as flags, anthems and ceremonies, the people of the nation generate social cohesion based on their shared national values and way of life. In this sense, individuals gain psychological and material protection from a sense of belonging. What is more, this security can be greatly enhanced if the nation is united with political power. This is where the idea of nationalism comes to the fore (35).

Hence, a further advantage of structures in this context is that they can become the embodiment of individuals' aspirations at the start of a new dawn, as some would refer to the years of African political independence. This is where *the issue of trust* comes in. There is however the need now to explore what agency is all about first.

Agency

The subjectivism of the agents is 'exemplified by philosophers like Sartre and sociologists like Schutz' (Chandler 2013). When we think about agency; action, rationality, and emotions of individuals are the defining factors of social phenomenon. Social interactions are not a pre-determined straight jacket for individuals to fit into. The focus here is on the subject which could lead to what Cotterrell (2011:6) drawing on Durkheim (1975b), calls an 'unconditional respect for the dignity and autonomy of all individuals by virtue of their common humanity'. There is an element of voluntarism that determines social reality. Giddens treats agency, not as the sum total of discrete actions but a continuous flow of conduct. There is an assumed understanding that individuals can be trusted to determine structures and not the other way round. This, however, is not the case for all schools of thought that underline human actions. One of its most full blown versions is in the form rational choice theory. Here, individuals are considered free, calculating and egotistic in their motives to engage in social interactions (Denzin 1990).

One of the benefits of rational choice theory is the self-interest that is its own explanation that needs no further clarification. However, as Boudon (1998) explains, the contradictions in different individual choices and the admission that actions can be non-instrumental question the very claims of the theory. More importantly for the purpose of the argument here, the egotistic dimension that could tear through structures borne out by individuals' actions shakes any trace of trust that any systems based on individuals' actions stand in the face of the proponents of structuralism.

The literature from African scholars is conspicuously silent about the active role of agency (individuals). However, this is understandable if one makes a deliberate decision to champion structure over agency. This is not to deny individual voluntarism completely. When referring to social order that African traditional laws maintained, both Mbiti (1969) and Tempels' (1959) above quotations refer to individuals, albeit as deviants to be punished if they failed to conform to the community binding rules. African traditional art is one area that can be used to make this point even more strongly.

Just at what point does the traditional African artist stop working on personal creative ideas and perfect his or her skills only to produce pieces of art that would embody communal values? Okpewho's (1977:309) analysis of the subject leads him to argue that,

> artists whose works enjoyed no patronage or adoption were doomed to oblivion, as their pieces crumbled with their homesteads. This situation has led art historians and critics to consider those pieces housed in a shrine or a palace, or else excavated in the vicinities of these, as the definitive output of the community, forgetting that much more that did not conform to the fashionable styles of the "schools" might have been done.

We can conclude from the above that individual Africans did have respect for traditional rules but they also made deliberate individual choices that would have helped or failed (been accepted or not by) the community. Likewise, the community would have set rules that helped or failed (were accepted or not by) the individuals. We cannot go back to pre-colonial times to prove the above point; we can however draw several examples from modern day Africa to highlight what is otherwise a 'winning and losing trust narrative' between structure and agency in Africa.

Trust: the go between

'Structure' winning and losing trust over 'agency'

It is hoped that the foregoing analysis of structure and agency has led to an understanding that both concepts have analytical values. They refer to different ontological perspectives. Instead of being dismissive of each other, both structure and agency must be recognised and that any attempt to ignore or abolish one or the other would be futile. Proponents of an exclusive and impervious dualism between structure and agency must however recognise that the prospects of one (structure and agency) ontological perspective gaining prominence over another can be said to be on the basis of *trust and security* that structures represent for individuals and vice versa.

Trust then is not a straightforward concept to understand. One of the key problems with *trust*, as stated towards the end of the first chapter, is our inability to penetrate human minds and confidently confirm their honest intentions. This *impossibility* is often replaced with *probability* or *improbability* of trustworthiness. Hence, trust is defined as the 'probability that he (structures or individuals to adapt 'he' to the argument here) will perform an action that is beneficial (…) is high enough for us to consider in engaging in some form of cooperation with him' (Gambetta 2000; Sapienza et al 2013:1313). That probability is the result of a process (of leadership) at all levels (school, hospitals, media, government and especially politics) as a commentary in *Political Quarterly Publishing* (2004:99) states:

It builds up slowly, but can dissipate rapidly under the impact of events (hence 'I will never trust you again'). It also functions as a kind of moral shorthand, avoiding the need for an elaborate moral judgemental calculus in our daily encounters with individuals, groups and institutions.

Africa is not the only place where trust seems to have eroded. In the UK, for example, the hacking and expenses scandals are two of the several examples of trust being (having been) broken between structure and agency. The hacking scandal involved News of the World Cooperation unlawfully and unethically accessing celebrities and politicians private voice messages. The expenses scandal took the lid off UK members of parliament's corrupt practices of fiddling with their expenses for personal financial gains at the expense of the tax payers. These incidents have damaged that *moral shorthand* that is *trust* between institutions (structures) and members of the public or tax payers as is commonly used (agency).

While new and innovative ways of building trust are being thought about in various quarters, an existing policy divide on taxation and spending and the political rhetoric used to caricature rival parties epitomises my argument here. The conservative party, for example, strikes the agency cord by promising lower taxes and community based initiatives and in that way be seen as trusting individuals to make the right decisions for their future. A small government then would relinquish 'state control' in favour of 'state steering' (Zambeta 2002). Without intending to do party politics, it can be argued that this is only part of the story. As already pointed out, individual actions can be egotistic, and investment in services of public interest (roads, hospitals, schools, energy, water systems, laws etc.) require not only further contributions but also a greater institutional involvement-which is the rhetoric of the labour party.

It is hard to articulate distinct political ideologies on the Africa continent but that is not to say that structure/agency and the issue of trust between them are inexistent. The era of political ideologies, as identified by Thomson (2004), is only a reality that emerged with the decolonisation of the African continent. African nationalism, socialism or other forms of ideology are said to have embodied values of unity, oneness and servitude leading to the banning of ethnic associations, other forms of political creeds. 'Nyerere, Senghor and Sékou Touré all stressed that there was a common ownership of the means of production (as all had access to land), while African leaders served rather than exploited their people' (Thomson 2004:85).

For Obiakor (2004:404) these are the patriotic leaders that Africa needs through 'the institutionalisation of a pragmatic system of African-centred education'. In Obiakor's world view, as indicated in the first chapter, this Afro-centric and patriotic leaders' discourse would represent a revival of pre-colonial or traditional African structures or systems and the values they represented. There is here an echo of consensus and shared decision making which is characteristic of collegial and participative models of leadership (Bush 2011). This however has to be understood in the context of existing hierarchically authoritarian forms of governance in various parts of Africa. The traditional African forms of structural organising may have had their successes and novelty in the values that they represented at the same time, but the purely altruistic leadership narrative could not be sustained in the face of what Thomson (2004) calls the crises of 'accumulation' and of 'governance' which led to the loss of 'the support of their citizens'.

There are several examples of agents (citizens) losing trust in structure (institutions) on the African continent, but two will suffice to illustrate the point.

In *The Unexpected Homecoming* (Elonga Mboyo, in press), is the first example where the author recounts details of how he fell victim of Oscar Kopongo Kabata, his mafia-like family's dishonesty in honouring a tenancy agreement in the summer of 2014 in Kinshasa/DRC. The victims had all the evidence pointing to either deliberate or ad hoc organised criminal activities. But to everyone's amazement, when the concerned parties turned to the authorities to arbitrate, the justice system exonerated the very people who had straightforwardly breached the contract. It could be argued that this is not an isolated case in the DRC and/or other parts of Africa.

The Anglo-Leasing scandal in Kenya is another such example. Following the smooth political transition in Kenya from Moi to Kibaki's presidencies, the latter represented the hopes of the Kenyan masses for real political reforms. The new regime, Bachelard (2010) argues, brought some significant reforms in the area of education and showed early signs of real commitment to restore the rule of law and fight against corruption. However with the Anglo-Leasing scandal, the Kenyan public and the rest of the world came to find out more about endemic corrupt practices that led to the award of a $35 million contract (and many more) to a bogus company that was not even registered in the UK.

Despite admissions by top ministers in Kibaki's government that they were involved in the scandal and that fees paid by the fake companies were intended to finance political campaigns, Githongo (the investigator) was advised by high ranking officials to drop his investigations and not to hand over his files of evidence to the Kenyan anti-corruption commission. Given the intense pressure that Githongo was under, he had to tender his resignation but published his report which forced president Kibaki to sack and demote some of his ministers but only to be reinstated later on (Bachelard 2010:191-192).

One of Bachelard's concluding remarks is that domestic and international protests following the scandal 'contributed to the socialisation of the population into the norms of good governance' (2010:196). To echo the 'diminishing support of the citizens towards their institutions' theme from Thomson (2004), Bachelard argues that because the population is more socialised with the norms of good governance, their support or tolerance for corrupt regimes will be diminished.

The support element is what is referred to here as *trust* which, according to Thomson, can be regained through *constitutional mechanisms* that are put in place in certain liberal democracies. *Constitutional mechanisms* alone, it can be argued, have a static character to them and they can easily be ignored. The view here therefore is that such mechanisms need to be placed within a bigger picture of on-going social construction which is exemplified through the duality of structures which is discussed in the latter part of this chapter.

'Agency' winning and losing trust over 'Structure'

In the interest of maintaining balance, the argument will now focus on identifying traces of trust narratives of human agency on the African continent. Not doing so would be perpetuating the same mistakes that Greenfield (1986:61) laments when he says:

by eliminating We have a science of administration which can deal only with facts and which does so from its consideration all human passion, weakness, conviction, hope, will, pity, frailty, altruism, courage, vice and virtue…in its own impotence, it is inward-looking, self-deluding, self-defeating, and unnecessarily boring.

In the context of African political systems, what Thomson (2004) calls a rejuvenated civil society could be used here as an example of the time of reckoning with human passion that Greenfield evokes. Thomson describes it with the following words:

Churches, trade unions, ethnic associations, women's organisations, professional bodies, farming co-operatives, community groups and eventually political parties, had all at some time played a key role in the fight against colonial rule. These same associational organisations would also contribute significantly to Africa's 'second liberation' of the late 1980s and early 1900s.

More recently, individual acts of discontent in North Africa that struck a chord with the general public and resulted in what is now commonly referred to as 'the Arab spring' can be viewed as the generalisation of what may have begun as isolated individual actions. The technological innovations in telecommunication in Kenya, individual philanthropic initiatives by the Multi-billionaire Mo Ibrahim and many others illustrate Africa's agentic ability to effect positive change on the continent.

However, the above rather salvific and trust inspiring agentic organising has not been replicated everywhere all the time. Letseke (2013), for example, gives a more up to date account of regrettable acts of indiscretions of human agency in South Africa. Echoing a theme of human agency and rational choice theory, Letseke identifies some of those indiscretions as in the form of violent crime, premeditated murder, rape, assault, homophobic attacks, police brutality and disregard for the rights of the minorities such as pygmies, albinos among other things.

One now needs to cast the mind back to the horrific killings that led to the loss of about 800,000 lives in Rwanda. In 6th April 1994, a missile hit the plane in which the then (Hutu) Rwandan president Habyarimana was travelling. His instant death triggered genocide by majority Hutus on minority Tutsis who were now blamed for the death of the president. Smeulers and Hoex (2010) represent the views of those who interpret this genocide as the failure of institutional structures with the following: 'violence almost immediately started in a very ordered and organised way, suggesting that the new power-holders had carefully prepared the genocide' (450/1). When attempting to capture the micro-perspective of the genocide, the authors carried out interviews in Rwanda that revealed 'social interaction among hands-on perpetrators and group dynamics provided better explanations of the genocide than widespread ethnic fear and hatred' (436). To illustrate the view that human agency, not just structure, has also let us down, Smeulers and Hoex's (2010) recount their Rwandan informants as saying the following:

'some of my friends became killers. What made them change was greed. To get something from the killings. Their main motivation was greed. (Prisoner Y). 'It felt secure in the group and that was a reason to join (Prisoner W) (444).

Smeulers and Hoex's (2010) perspective is not entirely new. In 2008, the Rwandan academic Jean-Paul Kimonyo had published 'Un Génocide Populaire' in which he demonstrates a greater involvement of human agency in the events that will remain as scar on the history of the Rwandan people and the wider continent. To reiterate once more, the view that Kimonyo (2008) advances is that while the horrific actions that resulted in genocide in Rwanda had received institutions/structural blessings or backing, there was evidence, even in the predominantly Tutsi populated areas, to suggest that there were social interactional motives that guided the atrocities that led to people killing their neighbours.

Unless things have changed now, but back in 1990s it was the Kenyan government policy that any citizen from West Africa especially those from Cameroon and Nigerian could not enter into Kenya except through Nairobi international airport. My Cameroonian friends who once travelled by land from Kampala to the Kenyan border had to be sent back. With valid visas, their only option was to fly into Nairobi. The reason for that, we were told, stemmed from previous individual acts of some West Africans dealing in drugs which made the Kenyan institutions to lose trust and make Nairobi's International airport the only entry port where they could, using modern equipment, effectively screen these 'dubious' subjects. Trust towards human agency here becomes a rare commodity.

Attempts to curtail such vice and broken trust on the part of human agency can lead to the prevalence of institutional or structural attempts to control and prevent any further mishaps. When done without the interaction with subjects in question, it can sometimes take the form of developmental projects (Arthur 1991) conceived with the intent of influencing institutional policy. There may have been improvements in how much government policies are founded or rooted on empirical referents (Howlett and Weelstead 2011) in other parts of the world. In Africa however, such empirical referents or a *real* agentic involvement is compromised by lack of transparency, corruption, clientelism, mismanagement of public funds and lack of separation between the ruling party/leaders and the state, an unfortunate side of a one party system that emerged for the intention of maintaining unity following independence (Thomson 2004).

Crisis of trust?

It will not be the first time that the phrase 'crisis of trust' is used. O'Neil (2002) voiced questions about trust in relation to the accountability culture and the 'audit explosion' in the UK. With the foregoing discussion in mind, it is legitimate to argue that the leadership crisis in Africa has been about 'a crisis of trust' between structure and agency with each presenting an unconvincing trust narrative. Mending such a 'crisis of trust' may depend on the choices of those people concerned in a particular social context. In most cases, the first initiatives have come from institutions or structures. After all, they are the ones that control various resources. Some initiatives (for example the audit culture in the UK) may be perceived as impinging on professional autonomy, but '*if they work*' in terms of transparency in the running of public affairs, it may not matter to some that 'targets, outcome-based evaluation, and bureaucratic form-filling in every professional arena has shifted the basis of professional work, trust and accountability' Lunt (2008:85).

In the light of the argument presented here so far, one needs to take a position with regard to how trust between structure and agency, especially in Africa, can be rebuilt. The position here therefore is that *'what works'* should not be imposed (accountability or other initiatives) by institutions on agents but any resolution for a course of action that is the result of structure/agency interactions. This is consistent with Giddens' duality of structures within his structuration theory that needs further elaborating.

Duality of structures:

For Giddens (1974:5), social reality is a recursive reproduction of social practices where 'structure is both medium and outcome'. One of Giddens' concerns, which is discussed a bit extensively in the methodology section, was the relegation of agents as knowing actors in a society or structures of which they are members. Aware of the unconscious and tacit stocks of knowledge side of human experience, actors are constantly involved in the 'discursive consciousness' and 'have some degree of discursive penetration of the social systems to whose constitution they contribute' (5). Stones (2005) argues, and it is also the view here, that because of the structure/agency interaction in the reproduction of social life, both structure-and-agency are present in the constitution of structure as medium and outcome. The constitution of social life, therefore, is not done by structure *on behalf of* agents or vice versa but as *a joint effort*. The same thing can arguably be said about leadership and just about anything including democracy.

Speaking about the spread of democracy around the world, Giddens (2002) notes what he terms the 'paradox of democracy'. What he means is that while new democracies continue to emerge which suggests the popularity of the concept and its practices, there is disillusionment taking over the old ones (meaning Western democracies) which is symptomatic of the crisis of trust. To overcome this 'paradox of democracy', Giddens suggests the 'democratisation of democracies'. By this he means: making democracies more democratic.

One criticism that can be made against Giddens is to suggest that the West is the epicentre of democracy, a topic that is discussed more extensively in chapter 4. Ayittey (2010:1184) refutes such suggestions and argues that 'just because there were no ballot boxes in African villages does not mean African natives had no understanding of the essence of democracy'. From Ayitteyr's perspective, duality of structures would even be an African concept for Africans to own and hold on to. But from various accounts (Bachelard 2010; Thomson 2004; and many more), it is obvious that government institutions have made 90 degree turn away (unscientific sampling) from whatever essence of democracy Africa may have had. An articulation of those very African concepts (democracy, and structuration theory in this case) is therefore necessary.

To return to the idea of 'democratisation of democracies', its parallel in Giddens' conceptualisation of duality of structures would read like: 'dualitisation of duality of structures'. While the idea of democracy and 'duality of structures' have to be conceived of in a relative way, they are

48

not a given to all contexts. Their existence is disputed and contested in some places more than in others.

Hence, the very idea of *democratising democracies* or *'dualitising' duality of structures* begs the question whether such a reality already exists and only needs evolving and developing. There are no easy answers or positions one can take without being labelled as either defending the cause of the elites who control structures by denying the people the opportunity to shape and reshape their structures or being seen as colonial, detached from reality and failing to recognise local efforts by local leaders to bring about duality of structures. It might therefore be advisable to simply rely on public opinion of individual cases to form a view whether a country, an institution or a field is an evolving duality of structures or not.

More globally and in the event that one identifies broken trust within a particular field in the way that has been argued here, the discursive joint actions of reproduction is what is proposed as the way forward that both structure and agency's broken trust narratives, especially on the African continent, can be restored. This sort of argument may be seen as a mere responsibility sharing and tension breaking strategy just in case joint structure and agency constitution of social life turns out not to embody and incarnate a people's aspirations. If we go it alone, what if things do not turn out as we expect them to? The 'what if' approach is a weak premise on which to base duality of structures and restore trust. It is self-centred because it has personal interests to think about in case things did not work.

The then Zaire case study adapted from Thomson (2004) illustrates to some degree some disingenuous ways to build partnerships to make them appear like genuine duality of structures. After systematically plundering the wealth meant for his compatriots, Mobutu (the then president of Zaire) witnessed a period where his citizens disengaged with his many governments, foreign powers disowned him and outside investors became reluctant to do any business with a bunch of corrupt officials. Thomson describes the final months or years of Mobutu's 32 year regime in the following words:

> Mobutu attempted to cling to power, despite the growing strength of opposition groups. Forced to liberalise the constitution, he still managed to stall his opponents with a series of political manoeuvres, including constitutional conventions, the postponement of multi-party elections, the funding of numerous bogus opposition parties, and by simply buying off opposition leaders. In the end, the country was left in constitutional deadlock, just as it had been at the start of Mobutu's 32-year reign. The president refused to relinquish control of what remained of the executive and the army, while opposition leaders in parliament failed to command the political strength to remove him (224).

The reading of the above extract is slightly different here. The contention here is that the Mobutu regime had been heavily reliant on structuralism. What counted was the will of the president through the institutions. Aware of his imminent downfall and worried about losing his grip on power, he began to ease the tensions and project an image of social reality that is shaped and reshaped by all agents of the country's society. Since it was started on a weak premise (that of retaining power for oneself), it had to resort to all sorts of malpractices (creation of bogus parties, promising and postponing constitutional conventions etc.). Any apparent cohesion was the result of agents being 'drawn into a process as ambiguous beings…they merely imagine they have reached power' (Freire 1996:108).

A strong trust restoring duality of structures is a form of coalition or partnership in the sense of 'an organisation of diverse interest groups that combine their human and material resources to effect a specific change the members are unable to bring about independently' (Brown 1984). It emancipates, educates, plans, adapts and takes responsibility. Whether we refer to them as advocacy, progressive alliances, or collaborations, the sort of partnership that is being advocated for here, through duality of structures, has an echo of Mizrahi and Rosenthal's (2001) conceptual framework for successful coalitions. The authors identify *conditions*, *commitment*, *contributions* and *competence*.

1. Among the *conditions*, the authors identify: political and economic realities; resources available within organisations; community climate and past experiences with alliances… and arguably the experiences of trust that both structure and agency have projected.

2. *Commitment* is more about the ideology that is based on public interest rather than personal gains in resources and power.

3. In terms of *contributions*, those could be understood to be the identification of both tangible and intangible resources that structure and agency bring to the table, their ideologies that need the investment of time and energy and the power to engage into action that would lead to specific goals.

4. On the level of *competence*, the authors argue for the analytical and interactional skills needed to achieve goals,

maintain internal relations and more importantly for the argument here, 'developing trust with, accountability to, and contributions from, the coalition membership base (Rosenthal and Mizrahi 1994)'. (Mizrahi and Rosenthal 2001:65-55).

It is necessary at this stage to develop and link the above concepts with the argument being made in this chapter. What it is not doing is to advocate for coalition governments or governance of whatever institutions in the sense that rival parties must be included in all structures. But that, such structures must reflect the partnership between structure and agency. As it is more explicitly articulated in the fourth aspect of the above conceptual framework, the unfolding of social reality that meets that criterion is what Echterhoff et al (2009) calls shared reality. In circumstances where there is not much commitment to duality of structures, and if anyone cared at all, the general population will get told what structure as outcome is projected to be or has been without involving them in the shaping or process of it.

The above authors stress the importance of process for achieving outcomes that would be part of a shared reality. In their analysis of the different dimensions when reality can be said to be shared, they insist that 'communication highlights a potentially important everyday mechanism underlying the construction of culturally shared memories and evaluation of the world-a basic mechanism for constructing social, cultural and political beliefs' (Echterhoff et al 2009:515). Those involved in that construction (structure and agency), they argue, need to do the following: 'rather than remembering or evaluating the topic information as originally given, the communicator will remember or evaluate the information as represented after taking the viewpoint of the audience into account' *ibid.* To effectively do this in a continent like Africa that is still entrenched in high levels of intimidation and autocratic rule, what is emerging here is the idea that is already advanced in the first chapter where it is argued that structure needs to demonstrate an *increasing sense of self-scrutiny* that should lead to a *decreasing sense of fear* in the population (agents) and encourage them to engage with the shaping of their social reality.

Conclusion

The influential work of Paolo Freire (1996) might be a fitting way to conclude this chapter. The distinction that the author makes between oppressed and oppressors in this master piece can be compared to agency and structure dualism. While the oppressed are portrayed by the author as victims of oppression and only cautioned to avoid dehumanising themselves by oppressing their former oppressors, the view in this chapter is that neither structure nor agency can claim the moral high ground given their respective failures as discussed earlier. We have a tendency of picking the lesser of two evils. The difference in this case, especially in the African context, is that those who control power and the means of production in these sovereign nations have no independent third party who would decide who is the lesser evil between: structures that they (the elites) have become inseparable with and the larger population (what for Giddens is 'agents' or 'the oppressed' to use Freire's term).

Embracing duality of structures could mean giving up on hard fought freedom from colonial oppression and this may explain the intransigence of both the remnants of independence fighters and newly elected leaders, on the African continent, have with Western critical views on their regimes which they characterise as neo-colonialism. In such a situation, and given all the state's resources that they control, structures are likely to self-appoint as the less of the two evils (between structure and agency). The imbalance of power therefore works in favour of structures (or the elites) whose media machines will claim that the social, political and economic reality that they are defending is shared reality between structure and agency. Such propaganda may be directed at outsiders whose interventions might be viewed as interference but it does not automatically restore the broken trust between structure and agency of a given setting (or nation). The concept of STRUGGLE comes to mind as central when thinking about African ontological identity (ies) but this is a topic that I come back to in the next chapter.

Restoring that trust as argued here would require the application of the duality of structures. And to borrow from Freire (1996), structure and agency would have to engage in a dialogical theory of action where communication is not the 'depositing of communiques whose contents are intended to exercise a domesticating influence' (112) but instead be based on true commitment to transforming action which 'cannot fail to assign the people a fundamental role in the transformation process' (107). Assigning others a role is as important as assigning oneself a role that effectively invites others to take up theirs. That can be realised with increasing self-scrutiny on the part of structures (or the leaders and the elites who are their mouthpieces) and decreasing fear on the part of the agents (actors or in other words the larger population).

Chapter 3

Duality of structures: a (not THE) methodology

Abstract

The argument in the previous chapter came down to identifying *trust* as a key element if structure were to win the upper hand over agency and vice versa. With examples of a tumultuous relationship of broken promises, it was suggested that rather than bemoan the conflation that structuration theory brings about, it was instead deemed beneficial to look at the value of mixing structure and agency in restoring lost trust especially in different fields (politics, schools, hospitals, police, etc.) across the African continent. In the first chapter it was argued that *Increasing self-scrutiny* on the part of leaders, representing structures, *and decreasing fear* on the part of citizens of African nations, representing agency, were the measures of the struggle for a healthier partnership between structure and agency in the light of Giddens' structuration theory. Based on those indicators, this chapter develops the thinking a bit further by seeking to identify where they sit within the whole ontological and methodological issues that might be encountered.

Introduction

This chapter discusses the ontological and methodological issues that could be associated with restoring *trust* in structure and agency social interactions across political, educational, health etc., fields on the African continent. Having become familiar with Antony Giddens' structuration theory from reading the previous chapters, there might not be anything new on the ontological argument. However, the methodological discussion takes the reader to new territory.

The chapter begins with parallel ontological as well as epistemological discussions that are consistent with structuration theory and the African worldview. On close scrutiny, the author argues for an ontological unity between structuration theory and African ontology (*ntu*). This is followed by a discussion on the methodological logic of enquiry and a brief overview of possible strategies that could be adopted when researching a topic with elements of duality of structures. Given the tumultuous and contested political and cultural environment on the African continent which seems to affect the way business is run in other fields, this chapter explores some pertinent ethical issues which could be minimised or avoided through a better understanding and application of duality of structures. The chapter ends with the introduction of (critical) discourse analysis as a viable option for data analysis.

Ontology

Grix (2002:177) argues that 'ontology is the starting point of all research, after which one's epistemological and methodological positions logically follow'. Like Grix, Blaikie (2000:8) regards ontological assumptions as 'concerned with what we believe constitutes social reality'. Giddens was dissatisfied with extreme dualism between objectivism/ structuralism and subjectism/constructivism. As ontological alternatives, objectivism or structuralism represents 'an ontological position that asserts that social phenomena and their meanings have an existence that is independent of social actors'. subjectism/constructivism with agency 'is an alternative ontological position that asserts that social phenomena and their meanings are continually being accomplished by social actors' (Grix 2002).

Stones (2005) distinguishes between 'ontology in general' and 'ontology *in-situ*'. The former refers to the abstract and the philosophical while the latter describes the substantive and empirical concept. His understanding of Giddens' ontology embedded in the theory of structuration reads like this:

> He (meaning Giddens) developed his notions of them (meaning structure and agency) in abstract terms so that the conceptual definitions he settled for would encompass all structures and all agents, the very nature of time and space. In other words, he wanted to capture the general characteristics of these entities so that the concepts would be useful to the widest possible set of circumstances across times and spaces (7).

With that characterisation of Giddens' ontological argument, Rob Stones hopes to advance what he terms '*strong structuration*' which is based on concrete empirical entities, ontology-*in-situ*. The position here is that, while discussions about ontological assumptions may start off being abstract, they remain assumptions which are impossible to refute empirically as Hughes and Sharrock (1997:5–6) contend. Giddens may have given ontological 'ideal types' (to use a Weberian phrase) of structure and agency that would be useful for the widest possible set of circumstances across times and spaces, but using Hughes and Sharrock's assertion these assumptions have a situational existence that is impossible to refute.

With the above discussion in mind, it could be argued therefore that the 'trans-situational' can only stand on the basis of real situational properties. Hence, *ontology-in-situ* is effectively built into *ontology-in-general*. Keeping the two together is not only consistent with Giddens' ontological argument, but also serves as a powerful tool to understand as well as overcome some of the ethical problems that one could encounter when engaged in researching the African social phenomenon from this ontological mind-set.

The differentiation in terms of *ontology-in-general* and *ontology-in-situ*, one might argue, is more of a technical exercise rather than pointing to a starkly different version of ontological reality. Besides, Giddens like any other before him thought of structure and agency as pointing to real entities in the conventional sense which could be represented by entities such as family, government, schools on the one hand and individual acts on the other hand. His *duality of structures'* characterisation of social phenomenon can then thought of, as Stones (2005:6) rightly does, as 'focused directly on the processes and practices involved at the point of interaction' between the conventional entities of structures and agencies. Research based on duality of structures therefore transcends this clear cut ontological positions and sees reality as neither nor but instead based on both.

Now, where do previous conceptualisations about African ontology (ies) fit into the above discussion about duality of structures? Are they far apart that it would render their apparent amalgamation far-fetched? While Africa cannot be denied its uniqueness and idiosyncrasies, denying that there can never be points of (ontological) commonality with the rest of the world begs the question about why we have African, Trans-Atlantic, transnational black ontologies in the first place given the multiplicity of African contexts. That would only strengthen the biased proposition that one hybridised discourse in the form of a collective African ontology (Puri 2004), often seen through profound cultural unity (Anta Diop 1962) and sometimes imaged as 'one cultural river' (Molefi and Kariamu Asante 1990), is more appealing than another hybridised discourse (seeing a convergence between African ontology and an ontology based on structuration theory). The proponents of a clear cut ontology divide need to do bear in mind the fact that 'the terms "Western" and "non-Western" (*structuration theory and African ontology in this case*-my italics) may (and often do) reflect biased and loaded assumptions' (Reagan 2005: 11). Instead of co-opting the clear cut Western versus African ontological assumptions, it is the view here that an ontological commonality/unity is demonstrable even if one started from the African ontological perspective – *ntu*.

African ontology is a minefield and we are nowhere near to reaching a consensus on African worldview whether opposed or similar to the Western worldview. It is worth stating that some of the work that have contributed to entrenched division in perceptions of worldviews (ontologically, epistemologically, axiologically and methodologically) have, according to Dixon (1977:121), failed to articulate or account for 'the origin, historical development, or the generic bases of the two worldviews'. Here, we will attempt to provide a generic ontological point of convergence between African ontology and the theory of structuration.

Focusing on the African worldview, the discourse seems somewhat territorial with the African continent and its intellectuals 'who never made the crossing' into North America being seen as playing a peripheral role in the construction of African identity (Bhambra et al 2014:294). This mutating field has prompted others to look beyond the *trans-Atlantic* slave trade and propose the *transnational* views of African thoughts in order to open the discussions to other experiences of collective black identity (Wright 2010). There are Africans who are not black and even blacks who are not Africans. We will use Africa and black interchangeably to ensure that no one feels left out.

African ontology or ontologies can be understood as a way of 'acknowledging Africa and the traditions of African thought' (Bhambra et al 2014) and being. If we look at structuration theory as an entirely western thought, African ontology would be about understanding social reality from an entirely African perspective. Only that, as we see it here, such an entirely African perspective is not far from structuration theory.

Let us assume that the 'authentic' African thought/identity has been obscured for several historical reasons. Those reasons may be about the Apartheid in South Africa, colonialism across the whole continent, segregation and racism that the black collective have and continue to endure and all their consequential impact on other social interactions. The non-territorial approach would be to see in the above experiences some commonality among those of African descent that crossed the Atlantic to America, those who remained on the continent and even those who, through other trajectories, constitute the African diaspora today. That common denominator for all the experiences of Africans can be put under the umbrella of supremacy and dominance. It is (white) supremacy or dominance that stands in the way of (obscures) African ontological identity. The STRUGGLE AGAINST that domination is deemed central.

Before we provide a response and prove how this relates to structuration theory, it is important to peddle back to the proposition that the sought after African identity is obscured. In some quarters, the emancipatory birthing of an African ontology is already a reality, albeit 'à priori'. Carroll (2014) makes the point that African view of ontology is essentially spiritual as opposed to the European one which is material. As a result, European Epistemology relies on the five senses while for Africans, knowledge can be acquired in ways other than through senses: spiritually. The author however concludes, rightly or wrongly, 'that due to the inability…to ground …work within a culturally-specific conceptual framework…a Black Sociology has never truly occurred' (Ibid 260). It is not the mission here to enter into a defence mode of Myers' (1987) work on which Carroll's (2014) argument is based. What must be acknowledged however is the fact that this is a contested field planted against the backdrop of STRUGGLE AGAINST domination and supremacy.

Without repeating the argument in chapters 1 & 2 and further illustrated by the forgoing discussion, the ontological thinking here departs from the idea of struggle (between structure and agency) and on that basis alone, *Africa through Structuration Theory - ntu* is rooted within the very essence of African reality. Whether the decolonising process leads to the excavation of an authentic pre-domination/colonial African identity is still elusive and the author finds such enterprise to be futile on the basis that you cannot step on the same river twice. Africa and Africans are not robotically static but rather dynamic agents capable of making conventions around values that they press into perpetuity.

The author wants to move beyond a selective and narrow understanding of struggle aimed singularly at a fixed oppressor (racist institution, individuals or colonisers 'of yesterday?'). The struggle must be thought more broadly first and foremost as one against oppression and dominance of any shape and form whether it has an Eastern, Northern, Southern, Western and even African label on it. In the wake of nation states, much of the struggle was against a moveable or displaceable occupier who the freedom fighters wanted to leave and return to their countries (Europe). We now live in a world where the 'oppressed' has also packed his bags and gone to live in the 'oppressor's' heartland (diasporan communities), or that oppression has been camouflaged in some forms of modernity (Bhambra et al 2014), through international and regional bodies.

Worse still, African nationalist institutions, which unlike the colonisers cannot be subjected to the same fate of being forced to return to a geographical space (Europe) they physically never set out from, have become predatory bodies. As it was illustrated in the second chapter, African agents have also faltered too leading to the loss of trust. In this scenario, the author's innovation, in line with structuration theory is to look at struggle not AGAISNT either structure or agency, but STRUGGLE FOR COOPERATION between structure and agency. The African ontology, therefore, cannot be divorced from the idea of struggle for cooperation.

Another way of conceptualising struggle is by use of the terms 'force' or 'force-beings'. 'The ontology of the Bantu relates to the key root *ntu*, and signifies force' (Smart 2008). Without seeking to (re) calibrate what has been said about

Ubuntu and other concepts with the *ntu* root, when Archbishop Desmond Tutu (2010:23) says 'in Africa, recognition of our interdependence is called Ubuntu', one cannot possibly limit that interdependence to only between individuals (agents). Structure and agency can be viewed as two force-beings not fighting against each other but intertwined in cooperation for a better future. If this *ntu* concept belonging to African traditional philosophy can be used to shape future ontology and the understanding of African social phenomenon, then we can possibly conceive of an African ontology that looks back in order to look forward. It therefore allows us to tentatively refute Gyekye's (1995) call for a separation between traditional and modern African philosophy and join a chorus of other Africanists who believe that 'our traditions are modern, our modernities are traditional' (Leonardi 2004:661).

The continuity from traditional to modern African philosophy must not be mistaken to mean the replacement of African structures, as defined by institutions themselves, in place of European ones. This Hegelian style is what is wrong with Obiakor's approach which does not articulate how our structures are to be formed and therefore leaves the door open for the exclusion of agency. Our traditions will truly be modern only when the modern African life is the result of a continuous intersection/interdependence between structure and agency (duality of structures) -*ntu*. We can express 'structure and agency ntu ontology' differently by means of Weibust's (1989) analytical tool for understanding traditions. It is to say that even though we may not be able to excavate the historical (African) traditions as in the content of what took place in the pre-colonial era, the *ntu* ontology of interdependence between structure and agency force-beings provides Africans with a mechanism to interpret traditions (in defining what they believe to have taken place historically and/or remain open to as well as seek to understand contemporary traditions (the way in which interpreted traditions and other factors such as modernisation, the need for skilled work force, increasing demand for value-based society, is manifested in people's lives today).

Rather than simply stating that duality of structures is the basis of one's ontological study, a discussion on how that translates into the epistemology and methodology in a given context is necessary. Before we engage into a discussion about epistemology and methodology, we need to push the above argument about *ntu* ontology a bit further. Let us hereby open a parenthesis on the concept of God.

There has been a divide between those who conceive of creator God as either the ultimate force being or of a nature far greater than and different from worldly force-beings (Smart 2008). On the basis of the argument suggested in this publication, we take the view that God for Africans is and should be a being of a nature far greater than and different from force-beings of the universe. To say that God is the ultimate force-being, is to suggest that s/he is the resolution, the point of harmony or unifying point of various force-beings. S/he is the perfection of all force-beings.

There is an attractive side to that sort of theology since it infuses Africans with the hope that they will one day be like God. The negative side of that is it postpones (pushes back) the complete harmony between structure and agency force-beings until the eschaton (the end of the world as a final divine event). Structuration theory then becomes one of Weberian ideal types which for Giddens (2001:14) are 'analytical models that can be used to understand the world.

In the real world, ideal types rarely, if ever, exist – often only some of their attributes will be present'. *Africa through Structuration Theory – ntu*, as presented here, is not an ideal type on the basis that only agents are first degree force-being. They are 'created directly by God'. Structures (institutions), on the other hand, are second degree force-beings in that they are the creation of agents (of the first degree force-beings). We take the view that God did not create communities of Africans (African governments, African Union, globalisation through institutions such as the United Nations, World bank… for that matter) but s/he created Africans who organised themselves into communities or carved themselves a communal worldview. Structuration theory, *ntu* ontology or struggle for cooperation is, in a sense, a reconciling mechanism between agents and their own creation (structure) here and now – and with that we close the parenthesis.

Epistemology

While the recursive-ness of social reality in the duality of structures may be an ongoing and stable process, what is reproduced is changeable unless structure and agency elect to place certain aspects of their interactions beyond their constant interplay. Some provisions in national constitutions in most African nations have this stable and 'objective' nature. Such rules that, according to Giddens (1979), enable and facilitate desired actions may project the nature of reality and the knowledge to be derived from it as a fixed entity. Structuralism is clearly embedded in the duality of structures. The temptation, therefore, is to seek to know structure which is both medium and outcome in a positivistic way, meaning being scientifically verified and proven. The positivistic charge is in fact what Africanists level against European epistemologies which rely on the five senses (Carroll 2014). In the context of ontology of STRUGGLE FOR COOPERATION between structure and agency, in other words duality of structures, the positivistic view needs to be tempered with the understanding of ontology-in-general being infused with ontology-in-situ. That means questioning and revising the doxa that Africans' knowledge base is only configured subjectively in a telepathic and spiritual realm (Carroll 2014). By bringing structure and agency together, one can argue that this is only possible within the framework of an epistemic interdependence between the two. Stones (2007) acknowledges that 'few assume today that there is a simplistic linear step-by-step model of the research process; one can tinker with each step if necessary to conduct enquiry' (271).

Therefore, the thinking that if one starts from a structuralist ontology he or she will end up choosing a positivistic epistemological approach and the same for subjective ontology for interpretivist epistemologies is problematic when faced with an ontological position that starts with recognition of interplay between structure and agency. It can be argued that the fact that one starts research from interpretivist epistemological standpoint does not negate the duality of structures which, as already mentioned, does not preclude the 'trans-situational' and the 'situational'. The challenge for researchers then is to devise a methodology that recognises the interdependence of both structure and agency. The next section attempts to do just that.

Methodology

'Methodology is concerned with the logic of scientific inquiry; in particular with investigating the potentialities and limitations of particular techniques or procedures' (Grix 2002:179). The main question, Grix goes on to say is 'how do we go about enquiring about knowledge?' (180). To answer this question one needs to explicitly show an interest in both structure and agency if one is to remain committed to a study based on duality of structures with an ontological interplay.

It was demonstrated in chapter 2 that in the world of clear cut ontological perspectives based on the structure and agency dualism, both structure and agency have sought to persuade or force each other to recognise their trustworthiness. Rebuilding broken trust means that for both structure and agency's actions to be configured as 'joint actions' they have to consensually overlap. To overlap in the sense that the very essence of structure and agency's actions is the power those actions have in inciting and inviting the other to recreate the social phenomenon within the boundaries of decency and civility. The decency and civility environment could also be conceived of as having respect to the rule of ethical laws and upholding basic human rights. It is only in this context that one can envisage appropriate sequence of duality of structures interaction. In 'post-conflict' and/or 'post-dictatorship' Africa, it is possible to envisage a nation seriously committed to the path of rebuilding trust and fostering ethically sound ways for advancing the economic prospects of its people, to witness moments where actors' *fearless* (intellectual or emotional) posture to engage with their structures is met, not with an iron fist, but with genuine and *increasing acts of self-scrutiny* on the part of the leaders who represent official institutions/structures. Whatever the change that is the result of this interplay is effectively structure as medium and outcome.

It was also suggested in the previous chapters that duality of structures was an effective way to restore broken trust between structure and agency in the unfolding of 'African' social phenomena. It was argued that, in the area of African leadership, the ups and downs of African leadership was the result of the neglect or consideration of human agency in what should be the interplay of structure and agency in the formation of social reality. Given the history of power imbalance where state machinery has been used to suppress individual agency, some African scholars have suggested different methodological approaches. One example will suffice to illustrate the difference with what is being proposed here.

The concept of Black radicals to manifest a tradition of resistance is taking hold in North America Africana literature. The idea highlights the audacity to speak the truth to dominating powers and consolidate a disparaging black identity (Quan and Willoughby-Herard 2013). What is crucial here is the authors' claim that speaking the truth to power 'offers a methodological resistance to the insularity and despair of some forms of nationalism while simultaneously attending to the crisis of the Black petite-bourgeois about their almost systematic compromises with whomever appeared to be the ruling class' (Ibid 111).

It is the belief here that the two indicators for duality of structures discussed in this publication offer a two pronged methodological approach which grounds the above claim. While we accept that speaking the truth is the right thing to do, one can only do that from a methodological position of *decreasing fear* from agents. *Decreasing fear*, in turn, can flourish (though not exclusively) if structure is *increasingly self-scrutising* or vice versa. These two methodological dispositions can be taken up as viable research projects. Let us take the example of the impact that the diaspora has on its homeland. It is perhaps the case that in an age of the internet, the diaspora's opinions will somewhat weigh on internal politics of some countries. What is well documented, however, is that direct tax payment to an Africa government in the case of Eritreans living abroad or hometown associations where help is directly channelled to family or town members back in countries of origin (Newland and Patrick 2004) can uplift the economics of a country. What a researching Africanist can do therefore is to assess the degree to which those diasporan interventions palliate the situation, make agents indifferent and tame their fearlessness on the one hand and implicitly justify, connive with or endorse some self-defending instead of self-scrutising structures.

There is another way of assessing *increasing self-scrutiny* and *decreasing fear*. There is a common sense view that if you want to know how people feel about something, you only have to ask them; or if you want to see how they live out their ideals then you only have to observe or study the trails of their lives through art, songs, and documents. This gives some indication as to the type of research that may be carried out. For example, there might be studies based on people's narratives, case studies, and phenomenological experiences that assess the above two indicators. Interviews, focus group studies, observations, artistic and text based analyses can be envisaged in order to collect data.

There is a plethora of literature on qualitative research methods and it is outside the scope of this chapter to discuss the ins and outs of what is involved in choosing this or that method in qualitative research. However, Marshall and Rossman (2011) for example, can be used as a comprehensive guide to issues in that regard. Instead, the focus here will turn to the seven categories that Marshall and Rossman use to underpin their discussions about qualitative research methods. The categories are particularly useful here when thinking about and preparing to overcome potential ethical issues of prime importance when carrying out a duality of structures inspired research in most countries on the African continent. Those categories invite a researcher to ask the following questions: what is the nature of the research? What is the relationship with participants? What is the direction of gaze? What is the purpose of the research? Who is the intended audience? What is the researcher political position? And what are the researcher's views on agency?

The African experience of agency still has some way to go before we can hope for not only the realisation of an authentic African ontology through the struggle for cooperation between structure and agency but also the production of knowledge in various fields. An agent (journalist and researcher for example) who is in a *decreased fear* mode would not only be encouraged to feel free to report and research the African reality but also be supported with the necessary resources and space. Unstable political environment in Africa, which we interpret to also imply lack of self-scrutiny, continues to restrict academic freedom and jeopardise the prospects of independent inquiry for the production of much needed knowledge for development (Benneh 2002).

The aforementioned questions certainly deserve a thorough examination by anyone considering engaging in a study that is based on duality of structures even if the researcher's answers to the above questions coincide with the views of those whose social phenomenon is the subject of inquiry. Finding answers to those questions becomes even more imperative when the subjects of a given study do not share the views of the researcher. In such a scenario, the researcher would be faced with thorny ethical issues that he or she has to resolve. The next section will discuss some specific ethical issues of relevance relating to worldview, power, ontology-in-situ catch and context in Africa.

Ethical issues and dilemmas

Worldview: The biggest problem in proposing an enquiry that is based on people's experiences is the degree to which their accounts are perceived to represent reality. Some of us want objectivity in what we claim and more often than not, we want convincing evidence that is devoid of any subjective perceptions which are subject to time, space, moods, ethnic and religious affiliations etc., Ontologically speaking, such an approach would view institutions (school, hospital, and all the cross-fields') as outside the realm of individuals and subjective perceptions. Another worldview might favour the views of individuals at the expense of reality as defined by structure. A third approach that is being proposed here brings structure and agency, objective and subjective at the same level playing field. Determining the nature of the research as being based on duality of structures (not to say ...*ntu*, 'struggle for cooperation' ontology) and sharing it with people that are not only the subjects of the study but also subjects who do not necessarily share the researcher's worldview can lead to *clashing worldviews, permission and access issues* that must be anticipated.

Reiterating the importance of worldview, Carroll (2014:263) argues that 'it is incumbent upon African-centred sociologists and social theorists to develop theories, concepts and models and produce research that is within the cultural parameters reflective of African descended people'. This publication responds to that by offering analytical framework(s) for researching and understanding African social phenomenon. Carroll's point however is also an indictment of the African scholar who has spent most of his/her time and energy fighting a fixed oppressor (colonisers and neo-colonisers) and by default absolved the nationalist oppressor/trust breaker (either structure or agency see chapter 2) instead of elaborating a worldview (based on various force-beings) towards oppression and transgression of any kind. An anecdotal and perhaps trivial example but nevertheless illustrative of the absolution reserved to nationalists but not to 'fixed' oppressors and those who have come to represent them is in the use of the 'derogatory' term *nigger*. A reference we black people are allowed, absolved to use on ourselves but would take offense of it coming from a white person.

Power: In social systems with *unequal balance of power* reflected through authoritative and paternalistic traditions, it might be threatening to question the very traditions that, they might argue, are holding society together. And even when access is granted, it is possible that researchers would internalise those (authoritative) traditions. When discussing the political situation in Rwanda, Clark (2013:38) for example, warns of the danger 'to internalise the logic of intimidation (inspired by a particular worldview), which means that many

72

of us (meaning researchers) self-censor'. Those who do not internalise the environment of fear may instead swing to the other extreme of power imbalance behaviour where the researcher is perceived or considers himself or herself as of a superior civilisation than the researched. A balance must be struck between conducting studies that (may be seen to) internalise either the logic of colonialism of the Western world or that of intimidation in some parts of Africa.

Ontology-in-situ: There is also the inability for individuals leading institutions to separate themselves from the very institutions they lead and this is consistent with Thomson's (2004) assessment of most African leaders. This, to some extent, is a repercussion of imagining ontology only in terms of *ontology-in-situ*. In this one sided understanding, not only are attempts to understand and scrutinise structures framed and aimed at people's personas, they are also viewed and perceived as attempts to expose the frailty of the individuals at the top of institutions. Without professional or political maturity or even emotional intelligence (Goleman et al 2013), it is possible that decreasing fear that pushes agents to scrutinise their institutions may resort to clashes between structure and agency prompting a self-defence response from those representing structures instead of self-scrutiny. Self-scrutiny is not about personal attacks aimed at leaders but instead about institutions in the way that Giddens uses when he talks about 'institutional reflectivity' (Beck et al 1994).

Context: The issue of context is drawn from discussions and defence that certain African leaders and academics mount to justify what they claim to be context specific ideologies or philosophies and therefore rejecting as 'out of context' Western based concepts by branding them as 'foreign' and 'colonial'. This ethical issue is highly crucial as it has the potential to unravel this entire publication which essentially uses a 'foreign' concept (duality of structures) on a completely different context (Africa). Given its seriousness which warrants a discussion of equal measure, the next chapter is devoted to exploring this issue under the theme of 'cross-context studies'.

Analysis: Once ontological as well as epistemological issues have been articulated, we are faced not only with ethical issues that have been answered, in part, in this chapter and the next. One is also faced with the choice of a consistent data analysis strategy that reveals the extent to which a field (nations, schools, universities, hospitals, businesses, media, governmental and non-governmental organisations…) is on the path to duality of structures through increasing institutional self-scrutiny and decreasing fear on the part of the population or members of any field. It might be useful to start considering (critical) discourse analysis.

It is essential to re-familiarise with the discussion towards the end of chapter 1 in order to fully grasp the coherence that discussion has with (critical) discourse analysis. In a nutshell, the argument that led to proposing *increasing self-scrutiny* and *decreasing fear* was based on the philosophical concept that privileged a shared implication between structure and agency in the shaping and reshaping of social reality. This was deemed to be a credible way forward given a long history of broken trust that both structure and agency had shown over the years. Conceptual frames such as the *conditions, commitment, contributions and competence* of Mizrahi and Rosenthal (2001) and the *shared reality* of Echterhoff et al (2009) were brought in to make the case for how duality of structures can be operationalised.

74

The right kind of communication in the formation of shared reality that is shaped as a result of duality of structures is essential. The duo *Increasing self-scrutiny and decreasing fear,* therefore, serve as synchronised pedals that structure and agency use to cycle back and forth to allow shared social phenomenon to emerge. In this sense, we are not only concerned with the way communication unfolds for its own sake but importantly with how it works to construct genuine duality of structures inspired social realities. Foucault (1972) believed that language can help produce the objects they claim to describe. On that basis, critical discourse analysis is useful because

> critical discourse analysts go beyond the rhetorical and technical analysis of language to explore its social and political setting, uses and effects. They see language as crucial to ways that power is reproduced, legitimised and exercised within social relations and institutions (Tonkiss 2012:408).

Ultimately, data analysis will follow from how people come to know and how they communicate what they claim know given the *decreasing fear* and *self-scrutiny* modes that they are in. It is possible, though beyond the scope of this publication, to imagine a multiplicity of analysis strategies based on data from African art, stories, narratives, proverbs, etc.

Double de-contextualisation: a methodological myth or reality?

Abstract:

Journalistic reports during the November 2013 visit of the British Prime Minister David Cameron to China echoed one view of the Chinese society (and perhaps of any other society) of Britain being a nice country to travel to and study in. Though this was meant to highlight Britain's 'diminishing' influence on the world stage, it can be argued that British universities are renowned worldwide and so are other universities in Europe, North America and why not Africa and Asia as shall be briefly alluded to in the next chapter. Yet there is a sense within communities whether in Asia, Africa or elsewhere that one needs to go somewhere else to get quality education. In the same way, it can also feel that one is at the centre of intellectual ideas to which the rest of the world gravitates. When intellectual concepts are said to be of a particular setting, they can be rejected by others under the same pretext and, hence, diminish their usefulness. We unquestionably either hand over or hold onto intellectual spaces. This chapter attempts to engage with underlying philosophical and methodological issues related to the complexity of cross-context studies, ownership as well as application of knowledge or theories that may seem close and yet removed from us or vice versa.

Introduction

This chapter discusses and takes a position with regard to what is termed here as 'double de-contextualisation' (particularly when engaged in academic research with implications on cross context studies). It begins with a brief definition of the central term (s) of reference. The following section provides a backdrop of instances when 'double de-contextualisation' may be prevalent and identify some emergent issues some of which being the stability and limitedness of knowledge. In the subsequent section, an analysis of possible types of knowledge or theories within social research when thinking about 'double de-contextualisation' in a complex world is given. It uses primary and secondary knowledge distinction to refer to those various theoretical concepts in social research. This analysis leads to the identification of one academic, Pierre Bourdieu; and an attempt to locate his *secondary* theoretical concepts, within complexity is made. What then follows is an analysis, positioning and perhaps a didactically empowering presentation of arguments that can be used with regard to 'double de-contextualisation'.

Defining the term (s) of reference and rational

This section explains what is meant by 'double de-contextualisation' here. According to Oxford English Dictionary, 'to contextualise' means to place something into context. McCormarck et al (2002:96) define context as 'the physical environment in which practice takes place'. This definition is one-sided since it focuses only on *practice* and as a result leaves out *theory* which also has its context. De-contextualisation is then used to mean when practice or practitioners are taken out of their contexts. There is also the reality when a theory is taken out of its original context, not simply by someone wanting to grasp it and in the process coming up with incorrect interpretations or distortions as is sometimes the case (Merizow 1997) but mainly by a researcher, who uses a given theory on a separate set of people or practitioners who do not constitute the original constituency from which the theory or intellectual idea was derived in the first place. In this instance, you end up with both theory and the new set of people (practitioners) the theory is being applied on taken out of their respective contexts, hence the phrase 'double de-contextualisation'. This entire publication is to some degree trapped in 'double de-contextualisation' debate since it uses the concept of duality of structures by British sociologist Antony Giddens and applies it on an African context. It is hoped that the discussions in this chapter would give this work, and others faced with the same issues, some ammunitions to justify its legitimacy.

Concerns about theories of knowledge, what social reality is and how we come to know it will continue to preoccupy those with an interest to understand their surroundings. Such interest could lead to research findings that are often discussed as part of researchers' (be it philosophers, sociologists etc.,) theories some of which make it to conferences, symposia, publications and university lecture rooms. The view here is that those concerns, relating specifically to how and why we use what is provisionally termed as *context specific ideas* to research our professional world are not spelled out clearly in one piece. This is not to say that significant and perhaps ground-breaking attempts have not been made before. Reiterating an earlier argument by Smith (1999) as well as giving it a personal convincing account, Sikes (2006), for example, calls for a rethink of current methodologies that continue to hinder indigenous knowledge and methodologies to emerge. Owing to their pertinence, some of Sikes' recommendations will be rehearsed here.

Briefly though, Pat Sike's paper is crucial in that it justifies an interest not only of the Western researcher in indigenous contexts but also makes one put into context an increased mobility in cross context studies as indicated in the abstract of this chapter. Drawing from her own higher education teaching experience, the paper is focused on what a university lecturer should do when teaching methodologies especially to those with 'otherness' status and most importantly questions the domineering nature of previous emancipatory methodologies that claim to give voice to the marginalised.

However, the paper seems one-sided in that the author's admission of the relevance of the decolonising methodologies movement is outweighed by an overemphasis on the need for 'othering' language of inclusion to promote marginalised voices in the world of research. The paper does not seem to articulate what positionality a student (indigenous or not) should take with regard to theories and contexts that may seem close and yet distant or vice versa. The concept of 'otherness' is also left unexamined which only strengthens traditional assumptions about the sort of people that are being referred to. Without committing this chapter to queer theory traditions which keep open to questioning just about anything (Creswell 2007), it is essential that the deconstruction process of decolonising methodologies also provides a convincing deconstruction of concepts such as 'otherness'.

It is the view here that cross-context methodological issues need to be seen against a backdrop of (myth or reality?) of 'double de-contextualisation' and complexity which affect *all* researchers. This chapter aims to contribute to the need to rehearse ideas that can then be used to justify various (academic) writings of 'foreign' students, even 'home' students or those engaged in studying 'foreign' ideas in their 'home' universities.

When (double) de-contextualisation is most common

This section sets the scene for when 'double de-contextualisation' might be prevalent and discusses some initial issues that ensue. 'Double de-contextualisation' then might be described as a typical problem associated with novices in their early years' experience of researching their social and professional world. On a personal level, it will certainly take some years of research experiences before the author is able to prove or disprove such a hypothesis. However for colleagues in a similar position, and even for seasoned researchers humble enough to admit it, the questions of contextualisation and de-contextualisation of theories and research target populations are a real philosophical as well as methodological issue to grapple with. Let us consider this first example from the author's diary extract (developed more extensively in '*The Unexpected Homecoming*' – in press):

I am from the Democratic Republic of the Congo (DRC), with a Christian background, French speaking, with two degrees in Philosophy and theology obtained from Urbaniana University and Middlesex University. Both degrees were taught through the medium of English respectively in Uganda and London, UK. With a Master degree in leadership and management in education, I am currently pursuing a doctoral degree in education with Sheffield Hallam University. I am using some of the theoretical frames that I have learnt, most of which are Western ideas, to research professional practice in the DRC.

A 'double de-contextualisation' critique would question the link that these frames would have on the DRC context. There is nothing intentionally glary here to be self-indulgent about but this biographical extract unmasks the multiplicity of contexts that we, as researchers or any other person for that matter, are immersed in and perhaps the difficulty of exclusively predicating certain ideas we hold to one of the following: religion, traditional culture, modern culture, African concepts, European concepts, DRC, Uganda etc.,

The talk about (double) de-contextualisation is particularly common in parts of Africa or (political as well as intellectual) quarters that legitimately continue to assert their African/black identity as a way of subverting colonial and post-colonial forms of domination. Both demagogues and genuine patriotic leaders/academics draw from an intellectual idea that defines black subjects as subjective entities that need,

to remain true to ourselves as black learners who know ourselves more than the others who claim to know us better. It is to remain in touch with our holistic selves

82

as African subjects of learning and creators of knowledge. It is to challenge Eurocentric mimicry and the seduction to become white (*or use Eurocentric concepts* – my Italics) in (*the African context* – my italics) the imperialist Western academy (Dei 2014:171).

The title *Linking Higher Education and Economic Development* where Pillay (2010) analyses the implications of three successful systems (Finland, South Korea and the state of North Carolina in the United States of America) for Africa would struggle to pass the Eurocentric mimicry test. Modern Western democracy, for example, would be seen as a 'foreign' concept that cannot work in an African context unless it is given its fitting African definition by none other than Africans themselves. Wiseman (2002:4), for example, notes that:

In trying to assess the relative importance of internal and external pressures a large majority of academic observers, particularly those who are African, have concluded that it has been the internal pressures which have played a major role and that external developments have, at most, contributed relatively modestly.

A theory that is used to understand Africa needs to have been developed by an African in mind as the Journal reviewer of the first chapter states: 'Why not use a theory produced by an Afrocentric theorist, like Molefi Asante, instead of one produced by Giddens, who certainly was not African in mind'. While the advice to 'preserve a creative tension' (Appadurai 2009:50) between a European mimicry that leads to appropriating imperialist practices and a domineering arrogance that sees no way other than that 'which the coloniser is in the colonised' (Sykes 2013 citing Geertz 1973) needs to be taken, further clarity is needed to the debate.

The above observations and now the slogan 'African solutions to African problems' can be used opportunistically by both overstretched foreign governments who cannot continuously provide resources that their own increasingly nationalistic electorates desperately need and the elites (representatives of structures) of African governments whose 'sovereign nation' mantra is often evoked to give them the space to define, perhaps singlehandedly and without the cooperation of the population, their African versions of democracies. In their 'sovereign nation' mantra, they disguise their desires to be national guardians who 'get their position and power from the fact that only they are capable of interpreting tradition's ritual truth. Only they can decipher the real meanings of the sacred texts or the other symbols involved in the communal rituals' (Giddens 2002: 41-42). Placing Africans at the heart of African problem solving initiatives is also about recognising the fact that in the modern age of increased technology and cross-boundary communication, our identities are a mix of different factors as illustrated in the above diary extract. Hence, an insular African context that needs to resist external theories and concepts needs to be reviewed.

Despite the complexity that we as subjects and ideas that we produce are in, we still worry about pinning ideas down and getting things contextually right. Even if one disputed the notion whether subjects produce ideas or ideas run through subjects, it would still seem legitimate to ask whether those ideas running through subjects are the product of specific contexts in their past or a product of a complex mix of variables. The author is wary of the view that despite acknowledging the problems with objective claims in social research, there is still a tendency that we and ideas that any researcher uses are or should be from what can be termed as 'cleanly objective' sources that have not been contaminated with any other variables or 'contexts' to use a less positivistic term. It won't come as a surprise by now that this chapter favours the idea of limited knowledge but only with a caveat that "one should realise that the claim that we cannot have complete knowledge does not imply that anything goes. 'Limited' knowledge is not equivalent to 'any' knowledge" (Cilliers, 2005:260). Echoing the view from complexity theorists, Cilliers goes on to demand that the inevitability of tension and difficulty we are in when producing knowledge be recognised, demonstrated and talked about. The biggest challenge then is to do so without compromising the paramount requirement for 'our work to be taken seriously and perceived as convincing' (Mason, 1996:165).

Looking back at the author's autobiographical extract, asking anyone in such a situation to recognise and respond to 'double de-contextualisation' can be received at different levels. There is first the level of the heart and emotions. Such a level would ask rhetoric emancipatory questions such as: 'why can't I use any idea I want to?' and 'am I being held back?' These questions are legitimate but they should only be a starting point which leads to further questions. The second level then is the reflexivity level which would not see oneself as being arbitrarily prevented from the use of certain concepts, which would run contrary to the world class status and an outreach embrace of most 21st century higher education institutions, but recognise that we are all caught up in the world of complexity that requires reflexivity. In this perspective then, even the most obvious 'home-made' concepts, developed by your typical African, French, English and German philosopher or sociologist, are caught up in the complex world. The following section attempts to categorise knowledge or concepts which should lead to the identification of a key anthropologist and sociologist (Pierre Bourdieu) whose, arguably complexity-bound, ideas have had a significant influence on other people's academic pursuits.

Knowledge and context: between durability and complexity/temporality

This section distinguishes between primary or conceptual knowledge as opposed to secondary or empirical concepts exclusively within social science research hence sidestepping the traditional positivist versus non-positivist knowledge discourse. The intention in coming up with some form of labelling is not to create another theoretical framework or set any order of importance in knowledge but to simply provide a terminology or a glossary that can be used when thinking about the justification of the use of certain theoretical concepts in the methodological (myth or reality?) 'double de-contextualisation' debate. Needless to say that the labelling could only be achieved by way of analysis of what currently exists as bodies of knowledge available to be 'contextualised or de-contextualised' as the title of the chapter suggests and not based on any first hand fieldwork.

In organisational literature, Ribbins and Gunter (2002) have identified a form of knowledge 'conceptual', or what is also referred to here as 'primary' knowledge that is arguably not based on specific contexts.

Primary or conceptual concept

Conceptual knowledge domain, according to the above authors is concerned with the clarification of (leadership) terms or concepts without recourse to empirical data from specific settings. Philosophy in general or some of its branches such as metaphysics can be said to produce knowledge that can be categorised as 'purely' conceptual. Sociological concepts such as *structuration theory* of Antony Giddens also form part of conceptual knowledge given their trans-situational character that Stones (2005) calls *ontology-in-general*. Computer generated artificial intelligence can be included for its claimed independence from specific contexts (Nishida 2008) though saying that is problematic in itself. Making it to this list, you could argue, are knowledge or concepts emerging from reviews of other people's works. The reviews add conceptual categories onto other works without recourse to direct empirical research. Even though, they too (might) depend on earlier empirical research by other authors. It is within reason to imagine that most organised educational subjects with a formal body of knowledge (Freidson 2001) would have literature reviews of this kind and some familiar examples when thinking about educational leadership research and organisational analysis are Ribbins and Gunter (2002) as already mentioned, Burrell and Morgan (1979) and etc.

Empirical or secondary knowledge

In contrast then, much of the work of empirical researchers such as anthropologists or ethnographers, for example, is based on carrying out field work which involve going out whether this is done virtually or by use of any media from the comfort of one's office or physically uprooting oneself from a familiar setting to another setting. I is inextricably linked to context and subjectivity. Secondary knowledge is used here to refer to theories emerging from empirical studies.

The next section will develop the argument on when to use either primary or secondary concepts. The focus for now is on how the French anthropologist and sociologist Pierre Bourdieu can serve as an example to demonstrate/illustrate the complexity with empirical or secondary knowledge. Anyone familiar with Bourdieu's works will be amazed at the creativity of concepts such as habitus, capital, field, doxa, structure, agency and the rest to describe the materiality and symbolic representation of the social world (better to say French society if we are to stick with the theme of contextualisation) as a result of his empirical or secondary knowledge based studies in France. Let us briefly focus on the theme of structure as a result of his analysis of the French state (1994).

Bourdieu and the state of France

The discussion moves backward from an analysis of Bourdieu's studies based in one state (France) to another one (Algeria) to argue for a link between ideas emerging from multiple settings. From observations of the way the French state worked with its arbitrary laws, especially the orthography of words, Bourdieu concluded that such laws became the norm that subjects would even display an agentic force in the form of protests if an attempt to change those laws that have come to define 'the categories of perception' (Bourdieu 1994:8) is made. The categories of perception are what he would call symbolic capital which relate to other forms of capital such as economic capital as physical force and field of power in relation to the formation of a state. Though Bourdieu uses these concepts only in his later works, we need to remind ourselves that his earlier work that emerged from field studies in Algeria provide a pivotal backdrop.

Bourdieu and that state of Algeria

Pierre Bourdieu asserted his credentials as an anthropologist after his successful first publication entitled *La Sociologie de l'Algerie* in 1958. Ethnographic data from his field work offered an insight into the lives of Kabyle peoples, power relations and most importantly the interactions between the state (French colonisers) and their subjects. Driven by an economic desire in the interest of their country, the French resorted to forced (or voluntary) displacement of Algerians, in gigantic proportions, to ensure that the colonisers gained access to the land. Given the intensity and harshness of the colonial and Algerian war of independence, Bourdieu (1958) captures the mood of resignation among Algerians saying the Algerians inevitably become reconciled and accustomed to a state of existence that was rather vegetative. Despite his failure to use the words habitus, fields and especially 'structure', there is a strong argument to think that Bourdieu's intellectual work in Algeria influenced our conception of practice being the result of various habitual schemas and dispositions (habitus), combined with resources (capital), being activated by certain structured social conditions (field) which they, in turn, belong to and variously reproduce and modify (Bourdieu 1984)

The point here is far from questioning Bourdieu's subjectivity and authorship, but rather to make the point that his original sociological thinking is entangled in the multiplicity of contexts. It is possible that a 2015 French researcher would feel free to use Bourdieu's concepts assuming closeness with them based on a predicate that Bourdieu is naturally French. Similarly, the use of Bourdieu's concepts such as habitus, capital and others may be challenged when used in an African context, for example, simply because he is French and that most of his concepts were fully developed after research conducted on France. However, as presented above, what is close may seem removed to today's French researcher and what seems removed from an African context may indeed be close to it if one considers that Bourdieu's theories could have originated from a different context other than France. On close examination then, it could be concluded that the idea of 'otherness' has to do with people *them-out-there* as much as it is to do with *us-here*. The main implication of this observation is that it would be academically, politically and culturally naïve to dismiss other approaches to life based on old perceptions of impervious and bounded nation state contexts. The pertinent question is then, what do we do with secondary or empirical knowledge that is rooted in the complexity of contexts? The following section attempts to offer some justified recommendations.

'Double de-contextualisation': a positioning

This section moves to analyse and suggest the approach to take with regard to the types of concepts or knowledge identified here when thinking or worrying about 'double de-contextualisation'.

a. How can we use primary concepts?

Echoing concerns by Schegloff (1997) when talking about the tendency for relativisation and perspectivalisation in cultural analysis, it could be argued that it is a misplacement too to import indeterminacy into stable meanings that primary or conceptual knowledge carry. There are trans-situational ontological concepts and categorised knowledge domains through literature reviews that empower us to analyse and develop our understanding of social reality. It is not a distortion therefore to argue for stability of meaning when it might be claimed that 'all' knowledge is limited, tacitly configured (Polianyi 1966) and even most literature reviewers would always be clear about the provisionality of their conceptual frames. What is being argued here is that knowledge may be provisional as new conceptual frameworks could render old ones redundant but they still remain stable in as far as they do not depend on the relationship between the reviewer's framing and specific contexts, hence giving a leverage of its usage by anyone in any context as long as the concepts and aims of the study are clearly defined. To partly answer the question embedded in this chapter's title then, it would seem that 'double de-contextualisation' is a myth particularly in relation to primary or conceptual knowledge that seems to have a cross-context durability, not to use a stronger language of having an 'intrinsic' cross-context nature.

b. How can we use secondary concepts?

In the light of previous discussions, this section will suggest the different approaches that can be taken with regard to the use of secondary concepts. Those approaches will centre around four key ideas: subjectivity, innovation, developmental learning and emergence of local theories.

1. *Subjectivity*: as already mentioned in the structure/agency debate, subjectivity is a fact of life. An essential part of that subjectivity is about not dogmatically rooting oneself to a situation but also about examining and questioning (some might say 'thinking outside the box') one's surrounding. This is the power of reflexivity where humans recognise the world they live in and acknowledge that their perceptions are subject to that world. Personal trajectories are the familiar/subjective lenses through which we see the world. An African as a subject can consider himself or herself as closed in his or her own world but the reality of modernisation and technological advancement is that we are increasingly becoming citizens of the world. In phenomenological research, argues Levering (2007:215) the "'I' and the 'world' are inextricably intertwined" and drawing from Heidegger's (1954) concept of *Dassein* (man in-the-world), he goes on to say that "human existence implies that man is not only bodily in-the-world, but is also projected in time. Man is not only 'now', but he is a unity of past, present *and future*" (p 217). Hence, even if some might think that their past and present have been sealed off from the rest of the world, there is no guarantee that the future will.

There are several ways of looking at Levering's observations which could justify the use of 'foreign' concepts when analysing and wanting to engage with social phenomenon in an African context. Under the section 'Researching for the first time' in this chapter, the author's diary extract shows how much the multiplicity of contexts that we inhabit and that it is only through such previously acquired experiences, language and theories that we can seek o understand the world. Another way of illustrating how reflexivity reflects through subjectivity is to say that the same failed past leadership practices on the African continent are having a negative effect on the present and the people who embody that negative feeling want (or seek for) other alternatives (theory and practice) to have a different experience in-their-future-world .

2. *Innovation*: Lash (1994) uses the impact specialised consumption has had on the way products reach customers. Firms are now producing smaller batches and at the same time having to widen the array of products. In the same line of thinking, it can be argued that due to globalisation, Africans are interconnected subjects. Despite the fact that the right for information is still being curtailed in some places, the technological advancement through internet means that people are not going to be satisfied with one (failed) way of doing things. Innovation through reflexivity is what is needed here. From the mind-set of innovation, concepts do not rule themselves out because they are 'foreign'. They do so only if they are not yielding any results on the ground after a genuine effort to get them working as 'agents reformulate and use rules and resources in a variety of combinations in order chronically to innovate' (Lash 1994:119).

3. *Developmental learning*: Unlike primary concepts, secondary concepts have so far been presented as not having 'epistemic independence'. 'Epistemic independence' here is the characteristic of some concepts to be transhistorical but not 'ahistorical and independent from the field of concrete human experience socio-political concern and action' (Papastephenou 2001:300). However, if there was no such awareness already, the writing of Freire (1970) is a reminder that human action, including research, should be guided

towards empowerment and changing practices. This consequentialist approach embraces theory, more specifically secondary concepts, with a presumption that they have not only some form of 'structure' beyond the local contexts but also for the potential they have to provide learning opportunities for those interacting with them in other settings. Instead of placing emphasis on what sometimes seems to be a purely theoretical distinction between primary and secondary concepts, the focus would rather be on the single, double and triple loop practical learning (Tobert 1999) that individuals as well as organisations gain as they engage with secondary concepts.

People have visions and strategies which could include dreams about creating something new or experimenting alternative strategies. These strategies could be of a different context but would provide several single, double and triple loop learning for I, you and others involved in the learning. The use of the concepts of duality of structures as it is the case in this publication and other attempts to use secondary concepts/knowledge in various contexts can legitimately be carried forward with the intention of adding to a researcher's personal learning as he or she engages in the research, the learning in team process of conducting an enquiry and how the enquiry contributes to knowledge.

4. *Emergence of local theories*: In a positivist one cap fits all approach, data collected from various contexts would often be used to test some generalisable theories. Glaser and Strauss (1999) reversed this overshadowing dominance of quantitative over qualitative research by showing that data can be used to construct rather than to test a theory. This grounded theory approach to research is not only decolonising in relation to qualitative versus quantitative, but

also a blatant admission of the importance that local contexts and its data play in the emergence of theories.

Sikes (2006:350) has attributed this decolonising egalitarian approach to:

- The impact of postmodernism and post-structuralism and the increasing acceptance of multiple realities and alternative world views, incorporating an awareness of how, as individuals, we each can and do occupy a multiplicity of subject positions;

- Ever-increasing commitment to the recognition and realization of social justice, equity and equality for all peoples, underpinned by social models of differences, society and the world;

- Enhanced sensitivity to the role of discourse in constructing and framing identities and relationships;

- Various consequences of globalization and of improved communications and technologies which have had the effect of shrinking the world and bringing people from far-flung places into closer contact with each other;

- The money-making activities and expansionist, philanthropic, equalitarian and democratizing ambitions of western universities as manifest in terms of increasing overseas student numbers both at home and via various outreach and distance learning programmes;

- The research-related and educative work of non-governmental organizations and development agencies;

- Growing numbers of 'new' scholars and researchers who themselves come from 'other' cultures, communities and backgrounds or who are differently abled; and of course,

- Guilt.

Conclusion

It is legitimate to recognise the power imbalance that historical events such as colonisation have had on the way that we perceive knowledge and research. This chapter does not deny such imbalance but recognises the complexities of knowledge generation in an increasingly globalised world. A level headed analysis has led to the identification of what could be termed as 'an epistemological circus' (see figure below) that both the traditional 'others' and 'non-others' can both use to locate and justify various writings, commentaries and research projects.

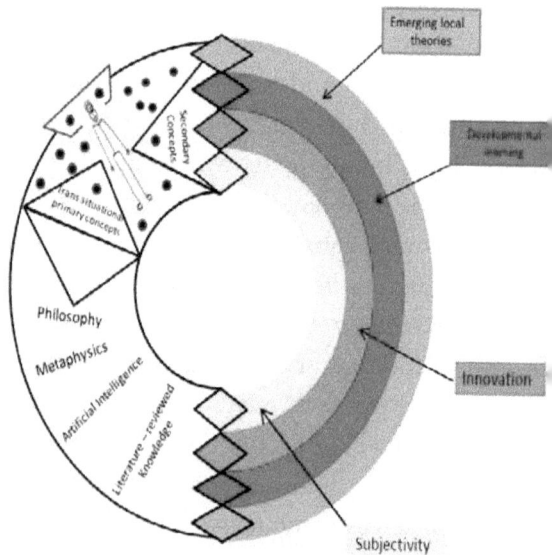

Image by Jonathan Kelly

The above figure attempts to summarise the discussion in this chapter. It shows the cross context student, researcher or anyone who still has what could be called personal or cultural values, knowledge, and methodologies plunged into a globalised knowledge circus. In that knowledge circus, there are concepts that are primary and others that are secondary. Primary concepts, as discussed earlier, are trans-situational and have an epistemic independence and they can be used or be applied to study and understand various situations. The secondary concepts are where theories are used for various reasons and purposes such as: subjectivity, innovation, developmental learning and emerging local theories. This framework is certainly not final but it is packed with ideas that can be used to justify various cross context studies.

With regard to the use of structuration theory in this publication, it is the view of the author that its use here is primarily as a *primary* concept. When framed as a *secondary* concept, the author uses it as part of his subjectivity and as an attempt for innovation to solve an enduring problem that was described earlier on in the preface.

Chapter 5

Higher education in the DRC and Sub-Saharan Africa: duality of structures in action

Abstract

A country's higher education can be seen as pivotal for human resource capacity building and stimulation of ideas for economic prosperity. Having been asked to help to formulate a programme of study for a potential upcoming university/higher education institute in the Democratic of Republic of Congo (DRC), a lot of questions, not least the relevance of a programme of the kind that was beginning to emerge for a post-conflict state, came to mind. This triggered a stepping back and considering of certain important issues beforehand. This chapter, therefore, reviews challenges that universities in the DRC and Sub-Saharan Africa face, analyses the current thinking about 'prestigious/world-class' universities and proposes local interactions, professionalism, lifelong education and quality assurance as the building blocks of curriculum development that sets the direction for universities/higher education institutes in the DRC and perhaps elsewhere in Africa. In retrospect, the new direction being proposed here can be framed as a practical example for putting the duality of structures into action.

Introduction

This chapter begins with a brief overview of the state of higher education in the Democratic Republic of the Congo

(DRC). This is followed by an outline of various non exhaustive challenges that universities in the DRC and perhaps Sub-Saharan Africa face. In the search for excellence a critical analysis of some internationally 'agreed' standards is undertaken in order to highlight what could be the strengths and limitations of such social constructs. This is followed by a presentation of the 2008-2009 objectives of the differentiated higher education in the DRC that the author was able to gather. These objectives are then analysed in terms of their strengths and limitations in the overall need for a DRC or African-based construction of excellence.

Extracts from the author's reflective diary which formed alongside the process of drafting a higher education programme of study in response to a colleague's request will be used. The extracts will include the use of subjective/objective pronouns and possessive adjective such as 'I', 'my' and 'me' to retain their originality and personalised nature. Taking all into consideration, the chapter leads to proposing a framework that a university/higher education institution in an environment such as the DRC (or others with similar realities) could draw from when thinking about curriculum/programme of study design and the direction of higher education institutes without jeopardising quality. The key aspects of the proposed framework, that shall be elaborated on later, are: local interactions, professionalism, lifelong education and quality assurance. The diversity of situations and the justification we all have for varying degrees of discernment mean that any given framework will not touch on absolute minutiae and it is possible that the reader may come away with more questions than answers. The view here is that such questions are quintessential since they encourage further reflections on the adequacy and suitability of envisaged solutions in different contexts.

DRC universities and their problems

Higher education is being perceived as an essential component for nations to be competitive in the knowledge society (Albatch 2007) and meet environmental challenges (Brock 2012). Hence, questions around curriculum and overall leadership of higher education institutions become necessary (Bolden et al 2009).

The DRC's higher education is divided into three parts: universities, higher technical institutes and higher pedagogical institutes. The total number of all the higher education institutes came to 776 by the end of 2009 of which 384 were public against 392 that were being privately owned/run (UNESCO 2010). Based on 72% response rate, there were/are more higher technical institutes than universities and higher pedagogical institutes nationally whether public or private. Between them, they shared a student population of 379,867. The country is enormous in terms of size and the total population is estimated to over 60 million people which may be similar to some European smaller states who count less higher education institutions. One could conclude therefore that the university and higher education sector in the DRC, like anywhere else (Jonasson 2008), is growing/expanding/evolving but not without its problems which are discussed below.

Jeongwoo (2013) argues that most universities in Africa, with the exception of some in Egypt, Kenya and South Africa, cannot compete and their chances of becoming world-class universities are slim unless dramatic actions were

101

taken. It is understandable if universities in the DRC were not included in that list. While others might see this non-inclusion as consistent with successive governments' shunning of their responsibilities (Titeca and De Herdt 2011), a long past history of conflict may be used to excuse current difficulties as the following comment by Teferra and Albatch (2004:22) might be (perhaps mistakenly) interpreted '… Somalia, Angola, and the Democratic Republic of Congo (DRC), have lost university-level institutions as the result of political turmoil and are trying to rebuild a postsecondary sector'. Regardless of the causes, they remain difficulties that need to be faced. The DRC state's absence in the primary and secondary education sectors (De Herdt et al. 2012) which has seen a huge decline in state funding is a trend that did not spare the higher education and/or universities. The longstanding underinvestment in this sector has led to what Mokonzi (2010:8) calls 'a recruitment freeze on teaching staff'. According to the author, 61% of the total staff does administrative jobs rather than teaching.

A high level of unqualified teachers is also responsible for the erosion of the quality of education according to the Organisation for Economic Cooperation and Development (2008). Quality however is only an implied concern in the list of challenges that the then minister for higher education and universities prefacing a 2008-2009 UNESCO's annual report on the state of higher education in the DRC identifies (UNESCO 2010). Those concerns are: state absence, proliferation of higher education institutes, ageing academic staff, poor infrastructure, lack of scientific equipment/laboratories/libraries, inadequate funding and poor governance. If we compare these with the challenges universities in Africa face, then one begins to see that most

102

problems are not limited to the DRC (Amonoo-Neizer 1998; Teferra and Albatch 2004). Amonoo-Neizer (1998:306) , for example, identifies the problems African universities face as ranging from reduced funding, increased university students' populations affecting quality, staffing, poor or inexistent research innovations to the overall relevance of the university as an institution given the growing unemployment rates which according to the author require 'continuing curriculum review and modification'. There may have been some improvement over more-than-a-decade ago since Amonoo-Neizer made the foregoing observations. However, the most recent one by Brock and Alexiadou (2013) is that Sub-Saharan Africa is the least developed region (in terms of education) in the world which means that universities still need to do more to play an effective role in the knowledge society (Albatch 2007).

Responding adequately to the above challenges or, in other words, ensuring that quality is matched with the quantitative expansion of higher education institutions, especially in the DRC, is essential. Amonoo-Neizer (1998) suggests adaptation, transformation, reformation and revitalisation. What these concepts mean in terms of curriculum design is not clearly articulated. Besides, the concepts tell us not only about the need for quality but they can also reveal different aspirations that universities have, including established ones in other parts of the world.

Before discussing the status that universities aspire, it needs to be noted that while some universities in the world go through significant transformation, they do so with the help of the state as education in most countries, if not all countries, will remain one of the basic services that a responsible government will choose not to ignore. In parts of

Africa, especially in the DRC, state absence in the education sector, in general, seems to have led to the proliferation of private higher education institutions (UNESCO 2010) and such institutions may have their own regimes. In principle however, the DRC's state and private higher education institutions have to adhere to certain mandatory objectives which presumably should impact on curriculum design and the direction they take. Those objectives will be outlined and critiqued here in order to position ourselves with regard to the direction universities in the DRC, and perhaps in Sub-Saharan Africa, should take.

In terms of aspirations then, they may be best represented in two poles. On the one hand, there are 'less credible' universities which do not want to be or would argue that they are not a failure. On the other end of the spectrum is the 'world-class' university (Jeongwoo 2013) status that does not come without personal, collective sacrifices and hard decisions to make. Mukonyoro (2007:222) uses the term 'successful universities' suggesting there being a staged trajectory in the overall drive to achieve the elite 'world-class' status. It is also possible that Isabel Mukonyoro uses the phrase 'successful universities' to mean 'world-class' universities. Whatever the stages or rather the diversified and differentiated state of the higher education sector, the criteria for a university to be classed as 'world-class' (Jeongwoo 2013), which are discussed shortly, seem envious at face value. However, a critique of those standards is vital in establishing the relevance of a university programme of study and the direction of higher education institutes, in the DRC and Sub Saharan Africa that do not or may never make it to that 'world-class' list but still be regarded as successful universities. The main question therefore that this chapter attempts to answer is: how do the DRC's and Sub-Saharan African universities define their programmes of study to secure the success that would justify their future existence?

Rethinking current understanding of 'Successful' or 'world-class' universities

World-class universities

There is no unanimity as to what constitutes a 'successful' or 'world-class' university. However, based on the global higher education rankings, Jeongwoo (2013) proposes four common features of those universities that seem to have propelled them to the top. The first is the *international dimension* which is often identifiable by the worldwide student population and outreach of the university. The second is the *intensity of research* that seems to co-exist with activities of an increased number of top academics in any one 'world-class' university. The third relates to the *technology and resources* that are not only made available prior to research activities but are also a by-product of their cutting edge research. The final characteristic is *genuine autonomy* that is free from outside control and interference in order for universities to engage in knowledge inquiries that seek the emancipation of mankind. With the exception of the last characteristic which is necessary so that decision makers can act on the basis of unbiased knowledge-base, the discussion in this section will focus on the other features in the context of universities in the DRC and the rest of Sub-Saharan Africa.

Rethinking the features/standards

The scale of 'huge investment which presumably might mean taking assets from other segments of the national education system' (Jeongwoo 2013:243) needs sustained financial and political will. The view here is that, with or without those huge investments, it is possible to imagine that some universities in the world may have reached the 'world-class' status in their own measures. However, the fact that such institutions are not yet recognised as such may not only be down to a public relations matter which would justify millions of dollars from those huge investments being rechanneled to website redesign, television and radio adverts by universities to raise their profiles (Brewer et al. 2002; Kittle 2000). But the author would also argue that the problem could lie in the flawed ranking system and conceptualisation of prestigious universities.

Brock and Alexiadou (2013:154) state, perhaps without elaborating on their position, that 'universities in this region (meaning Sub-Saharan Africa) and other poor developing countries are poorly served by the international obsession with university rankings'. An anecdotal way of interpreting the above pertinent comment is note the increasing numbers of African politicians who do little to improve their own universities but instead spend thousands of dollars supporting their children and relatives through those 'first-class universities' out of Africa. This has pushed some to take a radical stance, that may be financially unpopular unpalatable for those 'world-class' universities but liberating policy for millions of Africans, calling for a ban on African politicians schooling abroad (allafrica.com 2012). An alternative would be to put in place a reviewable moratorium on children of parliamentarians, senators and African government officials seeking admission into Western primary, secondary schools and undergraduate courses. And only admit them at doctoral level after a test and if they can prove that they have done an undergraduate degree in their home countries.

Let us return to the problem that university ranking poses. While acknowledging the need for African universities to engage with the reality of globalisation in its technological, economic and cultural dimensions (Amonoo-Neizer 1998; Mukonyura 2007), it has to be said that the categorisation 'world-class' is a social construct. The intention here is not to water down any agreed standards for defining what does or does not make a 'world-class university but instead to question the tendency to objectify not only the 'world-class' university standards we set but also the ways of achieving those standards. In so doing, we forget that not only can success be defined differently but also that it can be arrived at through other ethically moral means. The editorial by Acedo (2012) in the *Prospects'* special issue alludes to this question when presenting the ideas of one of the contributors to the appealing nature of 'world-class' education around the world. Acedo (2012:335) asks: 'whose voice is being heard? Whose are not? Whose discourse is it that results in particular standards, benchmarks, and indicators?' These questions do not only highlight the fact that 'world-class' university standards are socially constructed concepts, but they also strengthen the case for universities in the DRC, and Africa in general, to consider their positions and advance a coherent and credible discourse right from the conception of their programmes of study. The latter part of this chapter proposes one such discourse. However, for the sake of the argument, the immediate focus is on contextualising the 'world-class' university standards.

On the international nature of 'world-class' universities for example, Mukonyoro (2007:222) advances a subtly nuanced view arguing that 'successful universities are those that take seriously the needs of the wider society they serve as part of building bridges between the local and the global'. Seen in this way, a local university with local students can still have an international outlook and openness to it. The challenge for those defining the mission purpose and setting up programmes of study for universities/higher education, therefore, is to set the tone that is outward- rather than inward-looking. Though this can lead to increased national, regional and international partnerships between universities, private sectors and foreign governments and organisations that are vital (Jeongwoo 2013), it opens up important horizons in terms of importing and exporting knowledge systems (Mukonyoro (2007).

While 'successful' or 'world-class' universities need to be research intensive (Jeongwoo 2013), this factor is somehow linked to universities hiring 'top academics'. It is essential to have top academics whose skills in advancing the cause of science in whatever field cannot be stressed enough here. However, the global technological advancement in the way of knowledge sharing through books and online internet-based publications means that knowledge is no longer limited to the physical person inhabiting a specific institution. The challenge for universities in the DRC, therefore, is to make not only local knowledge but also global knowledge that is made available through various media more accessible in order to perhaps offset the brain-drain (Teferra and Albatch 2004) but, more importantly, to advance the vocation that Mukonyora (2007:223), citing Thomas Aquinas (d.1274), sees in universities as 'a place to learn about everything to enhance life in the created world'.

Looking beyond the religious nature (created world) of Aquinas' world view, there is an issue with the idea of universities being a place where you learn about *anything* or *everything*. This is worrying, and perhaps, a utopia for those universities especially in the DRC that are faced with certain challenges some of which have already been identified here. The lack of clarity around the above italicised word/concept can result in universities, in the DRC and elsewhere, setting themselves unrealistic expectations. While the idea of learning about *anything* is appealing in the way of enquiry pushing the boundaries of previously acquired knowledge further and deeper, the need for formalised and specialist knowledge (Freidson 2001; Larson 1977) implies that universities need to have a clear and well defined focus. Jeongwoo (2013:244) is therefore right in using the examples of Caltech and London School of Economics to point out that 'universities need not be comprehensive in their academic missions or be outstanding in all fields'. But even then, the author would argue that such universities do not learn *just about anything* in their chosen fields. Learning about *anything* has to be seen in the context of learning being a lifelong enterprise (Coombs and Ahmed 1974; Van de Veen and Preece 2005). In this sense, life as long as it lasts is where we learn about *anything*. Universities/higher education institutes then become places that equip students with the necessary (analytical) skills to understand, improve and perhaps predict the social and natural world beyond the confines of university establishments.

To revisit an earlier concern, the world-class university status seems to put universities in a *ranking* order rather than being in a *pool*. Ranking orders seem to work in such a way that even universities that are performing well are not given their due consideration as they may have been dislodged by others jostling for higher positions. Jeongwoo's (2013:239) example seems appropriate here to illustrate this problem,

> Malaya University in Malaysia, was ranked second highest, after China, among developing countries in 2004, but dropped from 121st to 201st (QS 2004, 2012). Therefore, while it appears that some developing countries desire to create one or more world-class universities, developed countries and a few developing countries are moving at a faster pace and taking actions to win the global competition.

It is outside the scope of this chapter to engage in a discussion about the Kantian transcendental argument or the Weberian concept of ideal-types. However, on the basis of the above citation, it is fair to argue that human experience is constituted in categories such as here and there, highest and lowest (Bristow 2002). Despite the fact that the ranking culture cannot be ignored since it has generated rich discussions about excellence, comparisons, economic development, it is questionable on the grounds that it seems to have become a profit generating enterprise for both the rankers and their regulators (Robertson 2012).

The *pooling* approach seems more credible in that it recognises both the diversity in our approaches to creating knowledge and efforts made by numerous universities without making them feel as second class. To what extend do universities integrate the above contextualised aspects of the 'world-class' universities' features will be the next focus using the official objectives for higher education institutes in the DRC.

Official expectations of universities/higher education in the DRC

Like most countries with a differentiated higher education system, this sector in the DRC is made up of universities, higher technical institutes and higher pedagogical institutes (UNESCO 2010). Whatever the conceptualisations in terms of quality, the view here is that excellence does not pertain exclusively to universities and not to higher technical and pedagogical institutes. However, for anyone wanting to set up a higher education institute, university or convert from anyone form to another, a coherent guidance that addresses the concerns raised here and enables silent voices to be heard in the overall discourse about 'world-class' education is necessary.

Based on UNESCO's (2010:18-19) publication sanctioned by the DRC government which the author translates (from French to English) below, higher education institutes have specific objectives:

1. Universities: They are responsible firstly for the formation of *cadres de conception* in *all* aspects of national life and with immediate relevance to the social and economic development of the country and secondly for the organisation of scientific research that aims to solve the country's specific problems and consistent with the evolution of science and technology.

2. Higher technical institutes: They are responsible for the formation of *cadres spécialisés* and *intermédiaires* both in applied sciences and arts as well as encourage artistic talents in line with the country's adaptation of modern information technologies, and

111

3. Higher pedagogical institutes: They aim to train teachers who in a general and specialised way will work to improve the quality of education by integrating a rethink o people's roles in society and through carrying out and publication of research.

Analysis

There are certainly various positive aspects from the above objectives that can be used to strengthen the case for excellence. The concern for national interests is high on the agenda here and so is a long term approach that intends to cover *all* aspects of the national life. The differentiated institutions also suggest that there is an awareness that *one size does not fit all* and that research was the engine for further innovation and economic development. It is however fair to say that these are not only aspirational goals but also partial in that they highlight a three-way gap that there is between these aspirational goals, the current challenges and the contextualised 'world-class' standards.

Without repeating the problems that DRC's (Sub-Saharan) universities face, that are not redressed in the above objectives, a consideration of how some of the aspirational goals for the DRC's higher education institutes may be counterproductive to the overall drive for excellence of the stated differentiated higher education system is necessary. For those grappling with essential questions about the relevance of any higher education programme in the DRC, they are bound to be even more confused about the definition of *all aspects* of national life. Here again, we are back to an earlier discussion about whether excellence can be defined only in terms of either *everything* or some specifically defined body of knowledge. Linked to this is the balancing act that might need to be negotiated between the highly prioritised national interests and international ones and impress its own different kind of national and international narrative of excellence. Until tangibly concerted efforts in terms of investments in higher education are made, public or private universities in the DRC and Sub-Saharan Africa will have to rely on a workable approach/philosophy that enables them to do more with less, as it were. Taking the foregoing discussions into account, below is an outline of an arguably manageable approach to achieving excellence, and perhaps write a different African-based 'world-class' university story. It is necessary to reiterate that the forth coming framework, which is entwined in the author's reflective diary extracts, comes as a result of the foregoing discussion. Given the limitations of current frameworks regarding 'world class universities' highlighted above, the author posits this framework as a viable alternative. The tenets of the framework are local interactions, professionalism, lifelong education and quality assurance.

Proposed framework

Research elsewhere recognises the need for *planned for* and *emergent* approaches to management of universities as well as curriculum of universities/higher education institutes that are reportedly complex organisations. At the heart of such complexity, that must be anticipated even in the case of universities in the DRC, is the idea that agents (staff, administrators, and etc.,) 'behave according to (their) own principles of local interactions' (Stacey 2000:42). While the local interactions may be very hard to penetrate, influence and regulate for existing universities that have had various individuals in and out of their institutions, that difficulty may be less so for smaller institutions in their early days. However, a more durable approach is necessary to turn the difficulty of complexity into a strength. This is why curriculum planning, and perhaps the overall conduct of business at higher education level, should be subjected to local interactions.

1. **Local interactions**: The internet and education mobility are empowering tools. One can just walk up to a renowned university or turn to google or any other search engine to get some tips on university curriculum and/or organisation that can be used in the DRC. While that is not necessarily a bad thing in itself, it only makes university organising in the DRC and Africa more complex than such institutions already are (McRoy and Gibbs 2009; Stacey 2000). However, since one has to start somewhere in designing a programme of study (or research projects), there has to be a philosophical recognition and practical strategy not to force ideas on people but subject them to local scrutiny and interactions. Rather than it being a one-off act, the process of local scrutiny and interactions needs to be a continuous exercise of assimilation, enrichment, adaptation and innovation as planned objectives come face to face with contextually emergent needs, realities and interpretations. Below is a diary extract to illustrate the importance of this point,

As part of my research in putting together a programme of study, I visited the web page of the department of education of the University of Laval (2014). I realised the university ran a programme leading to an award of a certificate in professional and technical teaching which counts towards a baccalaureate qualification. The main objectives of this programme seemed appealing and perhaps relevant to the DRC. However, the importance of local subjects' interactions was felt when my discussions with those I considered local people began to question the implications of calling the award a 'certificate' which for most people in the DRC refers to a primary school qualification. State Diploma is what you get after completing secondary education. A useful conversation followed on whether to adapt it to the context of the DRC and perhaps call it 'Diplôme avancé' (higher diploma) or a 'certificat d'études avancées' (certificate of higher studies).

Another way of underscoring the importance of local interactions (based on local needs) is in the area of research which is the driving force for (world class) universities. Let us take the example of research around 'water' in response to the needs of a particular African community. A research driven centre or university in an African community that has not got clean running water would prioritise research on drinking water treatment than it would on waste water treatment. This is not a licence for flouting standards for sustainable development but an attempt to highlight the importance of research based on local interactions/needs.

Whilst one might encounter rigidity and opposition to innovations, local subjects embody historical and ontological conventions which represent their interdependent identity with nature and the rest of the world. The emphasis here is more on the local subjects involved in the dialogue rather than the content of the discussions even though the two overlap. In the knowledge society, Hargreaves (2003) has

115

noted that while good educational institutions may enjoy some autonomy, those deemed as failing were subjected to intense performance training. The danger therefore is to wave internal dialogue and local interactions to rebuild confidence in favour of intense performance training of staff (Ball 2008) in universities (in the DRC) in order to transform a region that is deemed the least poorly developed in terms of education (Bock and Alexiadou 2013). This must be carried out cautiously and avoid destroying archaeological heritage (Arazi 2009), resulting into 'tenser relationship between humans and nature' (Fu et al. 2007:7594) and significantly (or irreparably) disrupt people's ways of life as well as damage their health (Wang et al. 2013). In this new light, one only waves local interactions at the cost of dialogue that is needed to build bridges with other knowledge systems and on many other levels. Therefore, setting mechanisms for local interactions is paramount in order to instil a sense of professionalism.

2. **Professionalism:** While local interactions privilege the interactions of local people who are directly concerned, professionalism here pays attention to what is/should be at the centre of those interactions and how the interactions unfold. The diary extract below illustrates the point.

I think that the DRC education system needs better teachers and primary/secondary school leaders. So a programme that touches on pedagogical and leadership theories and practices is important. However, a three, four or five year long programme needs further topics from areas related to teaching and leadership. I found philosophy interesting during my university studies, but (behavioural, developmental and social) psychology is also important for understanding children. There is however another factor: that of the DRC being a post-war country and counselling/psychology might be more useful for teachers to deal with whatever trauma that might be out there than philosophy or sociology

Questioning any given body of knowledge, defining the depth and breadth of formal knowledge (Freidson 2001) while recognising its tacit dimension are what might come out of professionalization that is done within the context of local interactions. The downside to the above extract is that though it takes context, presumably derived from prior (local) interactions, into account, it does not explicitly involve an input from other individuals which would have given professionalism a collaborative mode (Whitty 2008). Practical constraints for building collaborative networks/mechanisms and humans' innate ability to develop ideas anywhere means that (intense) training (Hargreaves 2003), as a way of updating others on what should be done, may define professional work at universities.

   Other forms of professionalism such as the traditional, managerial, collaborative and democratic modes have their strengths and limitations, at least in the settings such as the United Kingdom (Whitty 2008). That is why sensitivity to cultural practices that increase productivity while maintaining the un-biased nature of knowledge becomes an important consideration. The suggestion here therefore is for curriculum design and conduct of affairs in the DRC universities to be done while recognising the local interactions and (international and local) context-relevant knowledge systems. This is more likely to produce relevant programmes that lead to 'devotion to a transcendent value which infuses its

specialisation with a large and putatively higher goal …
(Freidson 2001:122). As argued earlier, the aim here is not to
make of the DRC universities places where one learns *anything*
or *everything*. In the context of scarce resources felt more so in
places that are already experiencing hardship like the DRC
and Sub-Saharan Africa, focussed and clearly defined higher
education *teaching that breaks the limits in learning* is essential
What is meant by *teaching that breaks the limits of learning* is
linked to the next key element.

3. **Lifelong education**: It was suggested earlier that
learning should take a lifelong character rather than be limited
to university lecture rooms. In some literature 'lifelong
learning' is an essential tenet where individuals can no longer
be satisfied with gained membership to a professional body
but endeavour to constantly update their professional
knowledge (Guile and Lucas 1999). In the context of
curriculum design and direction of higher education in the
DRC and Sub-Saharan Africa, a nuanced understanding of
'lifelong education' is necessary. Below is a superficial diary
extract to make a more serious point.

Many students studying at DRC universities have told me
that they sit on windows and even outside lecture theatres to
keep up with the teaching. If this has been a
funding/management problem that might take time to
resolve, then a lesson needs to be learnt and perhaps use this
example as a metaphor of learning being drawn out of the
established learning grounds into the world and life.

It could be argued from the above extract that teaching
should be tailored and programmes be designed in such a way
that learning is more focussed on the acquisition of lifelong
skills. Not only wanting but also being able to find out more
about the unknown social and natural world within a well-

defined area of study, reflections, and analysis that make up key aspects of methodological inquiry are essential here. Incremental subject knowledge base may be the by-product of such an approach to learning at higher education level. However, the ability to assess the strengths and limitations of one's stance toward the knowledge to be derived from both life's critical incidents (Cunningham 2008) and everyday occurrences is more likely to lead to both technologically and economically skilled people (Giddens 1984) able to transform living standards as well as mature generations that can stand the pressures of possible religious and cultural fundamentalism.

Adopting methodological inquiry in a wholesale manner is less preferred to enabling different indigenous approaches and innovation to emerge (Denzin and Lincoln 2008; Sikes 2006). This is not to say that external concepts and approaches cannot find their way in the DRC or Sub-Saharan universities. Instead, as the author argues more extensively in the previous chapter looking specifically at 'de-contextualisation', those being introduced to arguably 'foreign' theories, practices and methodologies should be able to articulate how and why they are using them.

4. **Quality assurance**: All aspects of this proposed framework are interlinked and to some extent local interactions, professionalism and lifelong education add to the quality of a programme of study and direction of a university/higher education institute. However, as a formal process, effective internal quality assurance that seems to be having a positive effect in some universities (Beso et al. 2008) is partly what is going to restore credibility in universities in the DRC and the Sub-Saharan Africa. Review board meetings, external examiners/verifiers, second markers,

reviews, standardisations, professional associations, licencing/awarding bodies and resource centres are just some examples of ensuring what Giddens calls institutional reflexivity, such that there are regular processes of loss and re-appropriation of everyday skills and knowledge (Beck et al. 1994). However, any institutional quality assurance reflexivity needs to be holistic, meaning inclusive of internal as well as external factors.

One can argue that an insular/closed educational institution is a thing of the past. The brain-drain challenge that African higher education faces (Teferra and Albatch 2004) is just one example to illustrate the idea that higher education institutes are systems that interact and are interdependent with the external environment. Any internal processes of conforming to standards and continuous improvement can be compromised by external factors and the DRC and the Sub-Saharan Africa have their specific ones that need to be understood and anticipated. Here are some examples:

The proliferation of private universities in the DRC and perhaps elsewhere in Sub Saharan Africa is an indication of the attraction that this sector represents to carry out the moral duty of educating the masses and perhaps advance personal financial benefits. However, the fight for institutional survival/competition can result in the dampening down of standards to keep student enrolment figures up.

Everyone has their own image of who (university) teachers/lecturers are. Here, a teacher/lecture is not viewed as a ruler who 'is free to do good turns for his subordinates, in return for gifts or dues' (Beck et al 1994:83). The following diary extract gives some background thinking behind this positioning.

Looking at UNESCO (2010) report, it is right to say that there are not enough academic and scientific staff in the DRC's higher education institutions. However, the few that are there have different other commitments. Some hold high profile posts in state institutions, various cabinets and political parties. A student in one of the DRC's universities once told me that he saw his professor once and for the rest of the year they had to make do with his assistants. Despite a student's best effort, you must buy teacher's notes and the assistant's practice notes if you want to stand any chance of success.

And the following from a concerned parent whose child attends a higher education institute in Cameroon:

> My daughter asks me for money to pay for her university fees and everything. But it seems like the quality of university teaching is purposefully sub-standard to force students to pay for extra, more serious and rigorous teaching sessions run privately by the same university teachers. It's like a parallel system.

Diminishing standards of living seem to have led to a trend where there is a constant demand for students to support staff financially which reverses normal practice of staff supporting students in lifelong skills and knowledge acquisition. Another factor to consider from the above extract is that, institutional qualify of any given higher education institute could badly be damaged by individual staff's success stories in the wider local environment that is competing with universities for ownership of expertise. While working to promote the kind of commitment that goes beyond the call of duty and discuss, through local interactions, professional ethical issues (Lunt 2008), it is important to consider the external needs of employees to preserve quality. Perry et al. (2006) is just an example in a plethora of literature on the theories of motivation. However, it is both the responsibility of universities and national leaders to work collaboratively in order to ensure that the wider environment does not diminish but instead improves the quality of higher education institutes.

The need for financial support to maintain quality in terms of paying staff a fair wage for example can mean creating and maintaining financial ties with private parties whose interests could relegate the impartiality of coded knowledge (Beck et al. 1994). The politicisation/spiritualisation of university posts can also compromise autonomy and the impartiality of science.

Conclusion

The main objective of this chapter was to reflect on what is involved in producing and sustaining a relevant programme of study for higher education/universities in the DRC and Sub-Saharan Africa. In so doing, the argument led to the setting of an agenda for the direction/leadership that such institutions need to take as they negotiate their own paths to success. The analysis has highlighted that excellence can be achieved through local interactions, professionalism, lifelong education and quality assurance.

Despite the author's best effort, translating (from French to English) the objectives that higher education institutions are set in the DRC may have had an effect on the accuracy of conclusions drawn in relation to their strengths and limitations. The lack of clearly defined guidelines from the

DRC's higher institutions on what is involved in the formulation of a programme of study is also a weakness not only of this paper but also of any university that has to operate in an environment with little or no guidelines on essential questions discussed here. Nevertheless, in authoring this paper, a (hopefully coherent) framework for action has emerged. This can be critiqued, enriched and used to support current and future adaptation, transformation, reformation and revitalisation work (Amoono-Neizer 1998) in the DRC and Sub-Saharan Africa.

It can also be argued that this chapter is an elaboration for the higher education sector of the thinking that is being promoted in first chapter *'African-centred leadership' and the theory of structuration*: a response to Obiakor'. It is argued there that 'a cross-fields' engagement with social phenomenon that is constructed through the interplay of structure and agency is what is needed' in the exercise of African leadership. Higher education being one of those fields, this framework (especially the first two tenets) therefore represents an overt way of embodying a healthy relationship between structure (universities) and agency (individuals that are, at least, directly concerned with their university's curriculum and future direction).

Acknowledgement:
I am grateful to Christopher Boxall for his critical readership and proofreading an earlier version of this chapter.

References

Acedo, C. (2012). World-class education: a response to global challenges. In *Prospects*, 42, 335-336

Aliber, M. (2003). 'Chronic poverty in South Africa: Incidence, causes and policies. In *World Development*, 31, 3, 473-490

Altbach, G. P. (1971). Education and neo-colonialism: a note. In *Comparative Education Review*. 15, 2, 237-239.

Albatch, P. G. (2007). Empires of knowledge and development. In Albatch P. G. and Balan, J. (Eds.). *World class World-wide: Transforming Research Universities in Asia and Latin America*, 1-28. Baltimore: John Hopkins University Press.

Allafrica.com (1st November 2012) *Students Seek Ban on Politicians' Children Schooling Abroad*, Al Bawada (Middle East)

Amonoo-Neizer H. E. (1998). Universities in Africa: The need for adaptation, transformation, reformation and revitalisation. In *Higher Education Policy*, 11, 301-309.

Anderson, B. (1991). *Imagined Communities*, London: Verso.

Anonymous (2010). West Africa Hosts Untapped Mineral Wealth, In *Engineering and Mining Journal*, 54-59

Anta Diop, C. (1962). *The Cultural Unity of Negro Africa*, Paris: Presence Africaine

Appadurai, A. (2009). The shifting ground from which we speak. In Fenway J. and Fahey J. (eds), *Globalising the Research Imagination*, 41-552. London: Routledge

Arazi, N. (2009). Cultural research management in Africa: challenges, dangers and opportunities, In *Azania: Archaeological Research in Africa*, 44, 1, 95-106.

Archer M. (1995). *Realist Social Theory: The morphogenetic approach.* Cambridge: Cambridge University Press.

Arthur, J. (1991). Development and crime in Africa: a test of modernization theory, In *Journal of Criminal Justice*, 19, 6, 499-513.

Ayittey, B.N.G. (2010) Traditional institutions and the state of accountability in Africa, In *Social Research*, 77, 4, 1183-1210

Bachelard, Y. J. (2010). The anglo-leasing corruption scandal in Kenya: the politics of international and domestic pressures and counter-pressures, In *Review of African Political Economy*, 37, 124, 187-200.

Ball, J. S. (2008). Performativity, privatisation, professionals and the state, In Cunningham, B. (Ed). *Exploring Professionalism*, 50-72. London: Institute of Education, University of London.

Beck, U., Giddens, A. and Lash, S. (1994). *Reflexive modernisation: Politics, tradition and aesthetics in the modern social order.* Stanford, CA: Stanford University Press.

Benneh, G., (2002) Research management in Africa, In *Higher Education Policy*, 15, 249-262

Bertilsson M. (1984). Review article: the theory of structuration: prospects and problems. In *Acta Sociologica.* 27, 4, 339-353

Beso, A., Bollaert, L., Curvale, B., Jensen, H. T., Harvey, L., and EmmiHelle (Eds.). (2008). *Implementing and Using Quality Assurance: Strategy and practice. A Selection of papers from the 2nd European quality assurance forum:* EUA.

Bhambra K. G et al. (2014). Contesting imperial epistemologies: introduction. In *Journal of Historical sociology*, 27, 3, 293-301

Blaikie, N. (2000), *Designing Social Research*, Cambridge: Polity

126

Bolden, R., Petroc, G., Gosling, J., and Bryman A. (2009) Leadership in higher education: facts, fictions and futures – introduction to the special issue, In *Leadership,* 5, 3, 291-298

Boudon, R. (1998). Limitations of rational choice theory, In *Chicago Journals*, 103, 3:817-828.

Bourdieu P (1984). *Homo Academicus*. Stamford, Ca: Stanford University Press

Bourdieu, P. (1984) *Distinction: A Social Critique of the Judgement of Taste*. London: Routledge.

Bourdieu, P. (1958). *La sociologie de l'Algérie*. Paris : Presses universitaires de France

Bourdieu, P. (1990) *The Logic of Practice*, trans. Richard Nice, Cambridge: Polity

Bourdieu, P. (1993). *The Field of Cultural Production*. Cambridge, UK: Polity Press.

Bourdieu P. and Passeron, J-C. (1990) *Reproduction in Education, Society and Culture*. London, Sage.

Brewer, D.J, Gates, S. M., and Goldman, C. A. (2002). *Pursuit of Prestige: Strategy and competition in the US Higher Education*. New Brunswick, NJ: Transaction Publishers.

Bristow F.W. (2002). Are Kant's categories subjective? In *The Review of Metaphysics,* 55, 3, 551-580.

Brock, C. (2012). Perspectives on the contribution of higher education to education as a humanitarian response. In *Journal of Comparative and International Education,* 1, 1, 13-22.

Brock, C. and Alexiadou, N. (2013). *Education Around the World: A comparative introduction*. London: Bloomsbury.

Brown, C. (1984). *The Art of Coalition-Building: A Guide for Community Leaders*. New York: American Jewish Committee.

Burrell, G. and Morgan, G. (1979). *Sociological Paradigms and Organisational Analysis*. Aldershot: Gower.

Bush, T. (2011). *Theories of educational leadership and management*, 4th ed. London, Sage

Carroll, K.K (2014). An introduction to African-Centered sociology: worldview, epistemology, and social theory, In *Critical Sociology*, 40, 2, 257-270

Chandler, B. (2013). The subjectivity of habitus, In *Journal for the Theory of Social Behaviour*, 43, 4, 469-491

Cilliers, P. (2005). Complexity, deconstruction and relativism. In *Theory, Culture and Society*, 22, 5, 255-267. Doi: 10.1177/0263276405058052

Clark, P. (28Nov-4th Dec 2003). The price of admission. In *Times Higher Education*, 2, 129, 36-41

Commentary (2004). The politics of trust, In *The Political Quarterly Publishing*, 99-101.

Coombs, P. and Ahmed, M. (1974). *Attacking Rural Poverty, how Non-formal Education Can Help*. Baltimore: Johns Hopkins University Press.

Creswell, W. J., (2007). *Qualitative Enquiry and Research Design, Choosing among Five Approaches*, 2nd ed., London: Sage.

Cunningham, B. (2008). Critical incidents in professional life and learning. In Cunningham, B. (Ed). *Exploring Professionalism,* 161-189. London: Institute of Education, University of London.

Dei, J. G. (2014). The African scholar in the Western academy, In *Journal of Black Studies,* 45, 3, 167-179.

De Herdt, T., Titeca, K. and Wagemakers, I. (2012). Make schools, not war? Donors' rewriting of the social contract in the DRC, In *Development and Policy Review*, 30, 6, 681-701.

Denzin, N. (1990). Reading rational choice theory, In *Rationality and Society*, 2, 2, 172-189.

Denzin, K. N and Lincoln, Y. (2008). Critical methodologies and indigenous inquiry, In Denzin, N.K, Lincoln, Y. and Smith, L. T. (Eds.), *Handbook of Critical and Indigenous Methodologies*, 1-20. London: Sage.

Dixon, J.V. (1977). African-oriented and Euro-American-oriented world views: research methodologies and economics, In *The Review of Black Political Economy*. 7, 2, 119-156

Durkheim, E. (1952). *Suicide: A Study in Sociology*. London: Routledge

Durkheim, E. (1975b). Individualism and the intellectuals, trans S Lukes and J Lukes. In: Pickering WSF (ed.) *Durkheim on Religion: A Selection of Readings with Bibliographies*, pp. 59–73. London: Routledge & Kegan Paul

Du Bois, W.E.B (1973). *The Education of Black People; Ten Critiques, 1906-1960*. Amherst: University of Massachusetts Press.

Echterhoff, G., Higgins, T. and Levine, J. (2009). Shared reality, experiencing commonality with others' inner states about the world. In *Perspectives on Psychological Science*. 4, 5, 496-521.

Elonga Mboyo, J.P., (In Press) *The Unexpected Homecoming*. London: Austin Macauley

Elonga Mboyo, J.P., *Keeping the Promise* (not yet published-please do not cite).

Fafunwa, A. B. (1975). *History of Education in Nigeria*. London: George Allen & Co.

Fafunwa, A. B. (1976). *New Perspective in African Education*. London: Macmillan

Foster, M. (1997). *Black Teachers on Teaching.* New York: The New Press.

Foucault, M. (1972). *The Archaeology of Knowledge.* London Tavistock.

Freidson, E. (2001). *Professionalism: the third logic.* Cambridge Polity.

Freire P. (1970). *Pedagogy of the Oppressed*, London: Penguin Books.

Fu, B-J, Zhuang, X-L., Jiang, G-B., Shi, J. and Lu, Y-H (2007). Environmental problems and challenges in China. In *Environmental Science and Technology,* 41, 22, 7597-7602.

Fuchs C. (2003) Structuration theory and self-organisation, In *System Practice and Action Research,* 16, 2, 133-167.

Gambetta, D. (2000). 'Can we trust trust?', in Gambetta, D. (ed.). *Trust: Making and Breaking Cooperative Relations*, pp. 213–27. Oxford: University of Oxford.

Gibson L J. (2004). Does truth lead to reconciliation? Testing the causal assumptions of South African truth and reconciliation process. In *American Journal of Political Science.* 48, 2, 201-217.

Geertz, C. (1973). *The Interpretation of Cultures.* London: Hutchinson.

Giddens A. (1979). *The Central Problems of Social Theory.* London: Macmillan

Giddens, A. (1984). *The Constitution of Society.* Cambridge: Polity.

Giddens, A. (2001). *Sociology,* 4th ed. Cambridge: Polity

Giddens, A. (2002). *Run Away World: How Globalisation is Shaping our Lives.* London: Profile

Glaser, G.B., and Strauss, L.A. (1999) *The Discovery of Grounded Theory: Strategies for Qualitative Research.* New Brunswick: Aldine Transaction

Goleman, D., Boyatzis, R., and McKee, A. (2013). *Primal Leadership: Unleashing, the power of emotional intelligence.* Boston, Massachusetts, Harvard Business Review Press.

Greenfield, T.B. (1986). The decline and fall of science in educational administration, In *Interchange*, 17, 2, 57-80

Grenfell M. (2008). Interest, in Grenfell M. (ed). *Pierre Bourdier: key concepts.* 153-170. Durham : Acumen.

Grix, J (2002). Introducing Students to the Generic Terminology of Social Research, In *Politics*, 22, 3, 175-186.

Guile, D. and Lucas, N. (1999). Thinking initial teacher education and professional development in further education: Towards the learning professional. In Green, A. and Lucas, N. (Eds). *FE and Lifelong Learning: Realigning the sector for the twenty-first century.* London: London Institute of Education.

Gyekye, K. (1995). *An Essay on African Philosophical Thought: The Akan Conceptual Scheme*, Philadelphia, PA: Temple University Press.

Hargreaves, A. (2003). *Teaching in the Knowledge Society: Education in the age of insecurity.* Maidenhead: Open University Press.

Hatch, J.M., and Cunliffe, L.A., (2013). *Organisation Theory: Modern, Symbolic, and Postmodern Perspectives* (3rd Ed). Oxford, Oxford University Press

Heidegger, M. (1954). *On the Essence of Truth.* Frankfurt: Klostermann

Hodge S. (2012). Guest editorial, *Perspectives in Public Health.* 132, 1, 16

Howlett, M. and Weelstead, A. (2011). Policy Analysts in the Bureaucracy Revisited: The Nature of Professional Policy Work in Contemporary Government, In *Politics and Policy*, 39, 4, 613-633.

Hughes, J. and W. Sharrock (1997). *The Philosophy of Social Research,* 3rd ed., London and New York: Longman.

Jeongwoo, L. (2013). Creating world-class universities: Implications for developing countries. In *Prospects*, 43, 233-249.

Johnson W. (2004). Never the same river. In *Proquest Education Journals.* 61, 3, 381-390.

Jonasson, J.T. (2008). *Inventing Tomorrow's University. Who is to Take the Lead?* Bologna: The Magna Carta Observatory.

Jones R. M. and Karsten H. (2008). Gidden's structuration theory and information system research, *MIS Quarterly*, 32, 1, 127-157.

Kimoyo, J.P (2008). *Un Génocide Populaire*, Editions Karthala

Kittle, B. (2000). Institutional advertising in higher education. In *Journal of Marketing for Higher Education*, 9, 4, 37-52.

Laplante, J., (2004). *Pouvoir Guérir: Médecines autochtones et humanitaires.* Québec : Presses de l'université Laval.

Larson, M. S. (1977). *The Rise of Professionalism.* California: University of California Press.

Lash, S. (1994). Reflexivity and its doubles : structure, aesthetics, community, 110-173, In Beck, U., Giddens, A., and Lash, S., *Reflexive Modernisation*, Stafford, CA: Stafford University Press

Levering, B., (2007). Epistemological issues in phenomenological research : How authoritative are people's accounts of their own perceptions ?, 215-226, In Bridges, B. and Smith, R., (Eds), *Philosophy, Methodology and Educational Research*, Oxford, UK: Blackwell Publishing

Leonardi, C. (2004) Traditional accountability and modern governance in Africa (conference paper). In *African Affairs*, 103/413, 661-663.

Letseke, M. (2013). Anchoring Ubuntu morality. In *Mediterranean Journal of Social Sciences.* 4, 3, 351-359.

Lomotey, K. (1994). African-American principals: Bureaucrat/administrators and ethno-humanists. In M. J. Shujaa (Ed.), *Too Much Schooling, Too Little Education: A paradox in African American life* (pp. 203-219). Trenton, NJ: Africa World Press.

Loyal, S. (2009). The French in Algeria, Algerians in France: Bourdieu, colonialism, and migration. In *The sociological Review*, 57, 3, 406-427.

Lunt I. (2008). Ethical issues in professional life. In Cunningham, B. (Ed), 73-98 *Exploring Professionalism.* London: Institute of Education, University of London.

Mandela, N., (18th July, 2007) Nelson Mandela and Desmond Tutu announce the Elders, theelders.org

Marshall, C. and Rossman, S.B. (2011). *Designing Qualitative Research*, 5th ed. Thousand Oaks, C.A: Sage.

Mason, J. (1996). *Qualitative Researching.* London: Sage.

McCormark, B., Kitson, A., Harvey G., Rycroft-Malone, J., Titchen, A., and Seers K., (2002). Getting evidence into practice: the meaning of practice. In *Journal of Advanced Nursing*, 38, 1, 94-104.

McKenna, T. (2011). Hegelian dialectics, In *Critique: Journal of Socialist Theory.* 39, 1, 155-172.

McRoy I. and P. Gibbs. (2009). Leading change in higher education. In *Educational Management, Administration and Leadership*, 37, 5, 687-704.

Mbeki M. T. (2001). African Renaissance and Traditional Leadership, In *Presidents and Prime Ministers*, 10, 4, 15

Mbigi, L. (1997). *Ubuntu : The African Dream in Management.* Randburg, South African: Knowledge Resources.

Mbiti, J. S. (1969). *African Religions and Philosophy*. London, Heinemann.

Mentan, T. (2009) *Democratizing or Reconfiguring Predatory Autocracy? Myths and Realities in Africa Today*, Cameroon: Langaa RPCIG

Mentan, T., (2015) *Unmasking Social Science Imperialism: Globalization theory as a phase of academic colonialism*, Cameroon: Langaa RPCIG

Merizon J. (1997). Transformation theory out of context. In *Adult Education Quarterly*. 48, 1, 60-62. DOI: 10.1177/074171369704800105.

Mizrahi, T. and Rosenthal, B.B. (2001). Complexities of coalition building; leaders' successes, strategies, struggles and solutions, In *Social Work*, 46, 1, 63-78

Mokonzi, G. (2010). *DRC: Effective Delivery of Public Services in the Education Sector*. Johannesburg: Open Society Institute for Southern Africa

Molefi, A and Kariamu, A., (eds) (1990). *African Culture: rhythm and unity*. Trenton, NJ: Africa World Press

Mukonyora, I. (2007). Globalisation and the university in Africa. In *Social Dynamics: A Journal of African Studies*. 33, 1, 221-223.

Murrell, P. (2002). *African-centered Pedagogy: Developing schools of achievement for African American children*. Albany: State University of New York Press.

Myers, L.J. (1987). The deep structure of culture: the relevance of traditional African culture in contemporary times, In *Journal of Black Studies*, 18, 1, 72-85

Naidoo, P and Bacela, P.A. (2012). Power and energy in Africa: a wealth of possibilities, In *IEEE Power and Energy Magazine*, 67-70

Newland, K. and Patrick E., (2004) *Beyond Remittances: The role of Diaspora in poverty reduction in their countries of origin*, Migration Policy Institute.

Nishida, T. (2008). *Situated Knowledge Management for Primordial Knowledge Model*, international conference on informatics education and research for knowledge-circulating society. IEEE

Obiakor E. F. (2004). Building patriotic African leadership through African-centred education, In *Journal of Black Studies*. 34, 3, 402-420.

OECD. (2008). The Democratic Republic of Congo. In *African Economic Outlook*, 241-255

O'Neil, O. (2002). *A Question of Trust. The BBC Reith Lectures 2002*. Cambridge: Cambridge University Press.

Olukoshi, A. (2006). African scholars and African studies. In *Development in Practice*, 16, 6, 533-544.

Onwudiwe, E and Ibelema, M (2003). *Afro-optimism: Perspectives in African advances*. Westport, CT: Praeger.

Okpewho, I., (1977) Principles of traditional African art, In *The Journal of Easthetics and Art Criticism*, 35, 3, 301-313

Papastephanou, M., (2001) Reformulating reason for philosophy of education, In *Educational Theory*, 51, 3, 293-313

Perry, L. J, Mesch, D. and Paarlberg, L. (2006). Motivating employees in a new governance era: The performance paradigm revisited. In *Public Administration Review,* 66, 4, 505-514.

Pillay, P. (2010) *Linking Higher Education and Economic Development*. South Africa, African Minds Publishers

Polyani, M., (1966). *The Tacit Dimension*. London: Routledge.

Puri, S (2004). *The Caribbean Postcolonial: Social Equality, Post Nationalism, and Cultural Hybridity.* New York: Palgrave MacMillan.

Quan, H.L.T and Willoughby-Herard, T. (2013). Black ontology, radical scholarship and freedom, In *African Identities*, 11, 2, 109-116.

Rabaka, R. (2003). W. E. B. Du Bois's evolving Africana philosophy of education. In
Journal of Black Studies, 33, 399-449.

Ribbins, P. and Gunter, H. (2002). Mapping leadership studies in education: towards a typology of knowledge domains, In *Education Management & Administration*, 30, 4, 359-385

Riessman, K.C., (2008). *Narrative Methods for the Human Sciences.* London: Sage

Reagan, T., (2005) *Non-Western Educational Traditions: Indigenous approaches to educational thought and practice,* 3rd ed., London: Lawrence Erlbaum Associates

Robertson, L. S. (2012). World-class higher education (for whom?). In *Prospects*

Rosenthal, B. and Mizrahi, T. (1994). *Strategic partnerships: How to Create and Maintain Interorganisational Collaborations and Coalitions.* New York: Education Centre for Community Organisation.

Sapienza, P., Toldra-Simats, A. and Zingales, L. (2013). Understanding trust, In *The Economic Journal*, 123, 1313-1332.

Schegloff, A. E. (1997). Whose text? Whose context? In *Discourse and Society.* 8, 2, 165-187. DOI: 10.1177/0957926597008002002

Schein, E. (1984) Coming to a new awareness of organisational culture, In *Sloan Management Review*, 25, 2, 3-16

Sewell, H. W. (1992). A theory of structure: duality, agency and transformation, In *Chicago Journals*, 98, 1: 1-29

Sikes, P. (2006). Decolonising research and methodologies: indigenous people and cross-cultural contexts. In *Pedagogy, Culture & Society*, 14, 3, 349-358.

Sikes, P. (2013). Working together for critical research ethics. In *Compare: A Journal of Comparative and International Education*, 43, 4, 516-536.

Smeulers, A. and Hoex, L. (2010). Studying the micro-dynamics of the Rwandan genocide, In *Brit. J. Criminol* 50, 435-454

Smith, J., Flowers, P., and Larkin, M. (2009). *Interpretative Phenomenological Analysis: Theory, method and research.* London: Sage.

Smith, L. T. (1999) *Decolonizing Methodologies: Research and indigenous peoples.* London: Zed Books.

Stacey, R.D. (2000). *Complex Responsive Processes in Organizations: Learning and knowledge creation (complexity and emergence in organizations).* London: Routledge

Stone, L. (2007). US graduate study in educational research: From methodology to potential totalization (265-282), In Bridges, D. and Smith, R. (eds). *Philosophy, Methodology and Educational Research*, Oxford, Blackwell Publishing.

Stones, R. (2005). *Structuration Theory.* Basingstoke: Palgrave Macmillan Routledge.

Teferra, D. and Albatch, P. G. (2004). African higher education: Challenges for the 21st century. In *Higher Education,* 47, 21-50.

Tempels, P. (1959). *Bantu: Philosophy*. Paris: Presence Africaine.

Thomson, A. (2004). *An Introduction to African Politics*. London: Routledge.

Titeca, K. and De Herdt, T. (2011). Real governance beyond the 'failed-sate': Negotiating education in the Democratic Republic of the Congo. In *Africa Affairs,* 110, 439, 213-231.

Tonkiss, F. (2012). Discourse analysis, 405-423. In Clive S. (ed). *Researching Society and Culture*, 3rd ed., London: Sage.

Torbert, W.R (1999). The distinctive questions development action inquiry asks. In *Management Learning*, 30, 189-206.

Tobert, W.R (2001). The practice of action enquiry. In Reason P. & Bradbury H. (eds). *Handbook of Action Research*, 250-260. London: Sage

Tsand, W.K.E., and Williams N.J., (2012) Generalisation and induction: misconceptions, clarifications, and a clarification of induction, In *MIS Quarterly*, 36, 3, 729-748.

Tutu, D., (2010) Ubuntu: the essence of humanity, In *Amnesty International*, 37, 4, 23

Udokang, L.E., (2014) Traditional ethics and social order: A study in African philosophy, In *Cross-Cultural Communication*, 10, 6, 226-270

UNESCO. (2010). *Annuaire Statistique de l'enseignement Supérieur et Universitaire : Année Académique 2008-2009.*

Université Laval. (2014). Certificat en Enseignement Professional et Technique. Accessed February 5, 2014 at http://www.fse.ulaval.ca/prog/c-ept-ept/bref/

Van de Veen, R. and Preece, J. (2005). Poverty reduction and adult education, beyond basic education. In *International Journal of Lifelong Education*. 24 5, 381-391.

Wang, Y., Xu, L., and Jones, B.J. (2013). The effect of the Chinese cultural revolution and great leap forward on the prevalence of myopia. In *European Journal of Epistemology*, 28,12, 1001-1004.

Weibust, P. (1989). Tradition as process: creating contemporary tradition in a rural Norwegian school and community, In *International Journal of Qualitative Studies in Education* 2, 2, 107-122

Whitty, G. (2008). Changing modes of teacher professionalism: Traditional, managerial, collaborative and democratic, In Cunningham, B. (Ed). *Exploring Professionalism*,28-59. London: Institute of Education, University of London.

Wilson, A. (1992). *Awakening the Natural Genius of Black Children*. New York: African World InfoSystem.

Wisema, J.A (2002). The movement towards democracy: global, continental and state perspectives, In Wiseman, J.A (ed). *Democracy and Political Change in Sub-Saharan Africa*, London, Routledge. 1-10

Wright M.M. (2010) Black in time: exploring new ontologies, new dimensions, new epistemologies of the African Diaspora, In *Transforming Anthropology*, 18, 1, 70-73

Zambeta, E. (2002). Modernisation of educational governance in Greece: from state control to state steering, In *European Educational Research Journal*, 1, 637-655.

Index

141

www.ingramcontent.com/pod-product-compliance
Lightning Source LLC
Chambersburg PA
CBHW071028280326
41935CB00011B/1492